Momma, You Don't Heal

June K. Collins

Table of Contents

Dedication:

To my beautiful daughter Bella.

You will never know the impact your life has on the person I am today.

Thank you for saving me.

In memory of:

Kaleb Giovanni Owens

November 26, 2009–March 20, 2012

Acknowledgments

I have always skipped over this part of a book. But now, after completing my first book—yeah, there are a lot of people to be thankful for. As I began this journey, I was encouraged by so many people to keep going. With their loving encouragement, I am here right now.

First, I would not be anywhere in life without my parents, John and Patrice Kraholik. You always said I could do anything and always encouraged and accepted me for exactly who I was. Although my mom did not get to see the finished book, I know she smiles down with my Kaleb at this accomplishment.

To my daughter, Isabella. My life was not complete until you came into it. God knew what he was doing when he gave me a girl like you. You saved my life from the hell I was living, just by being *you*. I will always live as free-spirited as you and make you proud. Follow your dreams no matter how big, because you just might accomplish exactly what you dream of.

To my son, Kaleb, thank you for showing me how to be a Momma and what unconditional love is. Through your trials and strength, you taught me how strong someone could be. I am a better person because of your life and death.

To all my friends and family, thank you to those who stood by me and have known me before Kaleb's death and after. Without the strong support, I would not be who I am today. To all my friends and family that I have grown to love since Kaleb's death, thank you for always being there and loving my Kaleb, even though you never met him.

On this journey, I decided since the book was for women, I would mostly have women perfecting it—even down to the quotes included.

So, thank you to all of you strong women. Without you, this would not be possible.

Introduction:

Momma, You Don't Heal

Congratulations, Momma? You are part of a club no one ever asks to be in and part of a group of women who are treated like they have the plague. Yes, you are a Momma of an angel, a child that left way too soon. The day your child left this world was the day your life stopped making sense.

Being a woman who has lost a child, you don't know where to start; but you know you can't stay where you currently are. Your mind is spinning, and you probably have guilt, along with fear of the future. And let's not even talk about the loneliness... being surrounded by several people (if not hundreds) and feeling as if you are the only person there. Well Mom, you kinda are, unless by chance you have another person with you who has lost a child. Losing a child is one of the loneliest paths you will travel, and the world will make you feel there is only one path you have to take. We feel silenced to dwell in our own sorrow, because if we speak about our loss, we learn it is either awkward or others don't want to hear about it.

My story is a hard one to tell, one with many ups and downs. I can remember the first days of my loss. I can remember being surrounded by so many people but feeling the loneliest I had ever felt. In my life. I can remember every detail, even down to what my child was wearing the day he passed away. I don't think those memories ever go away, they are etched into our brain forever.

I think we expect that we are one day going to wake up and just be okay. That there is a "healing," and we are going to go back to normal—back to the way it once was. I've never been good at sugarcoating anything, so I'm going to be honest. There is no healing from child loss. To even suggest that anyone would frame the term "healing" with child loss is ludicrous. News flash, I have said the obvious: Ladies, we don't heal, we learn to *deal* with our child loss.

Dealing with it is the simplest way to describe it. We learn how to deal with our thoughts, deal with people, and deal with our life in general. We learn what we will and will *not* deal with in our life. It's a lot of learning and discovering after child loss, but please know this: You can be happy again, and you can survive your loss. I have been there Mommas, and I am living proof. This is coming from an ordinary mom, with an ordinary life. I am not a celebrity, nor have I ever met one. There are no fancy frills with me, just the truth I want to share with all of you.

It's been 11 years since my Kaleb died, and there isn't a day that goes by that I don't think of him. He is as much a part of my life now as he was when he was here with me. One day, I made a decision: I could not live life for the next 30, 40, or 50 years like I was living... I was only 31 when Kaleb died. I didn't know what to do or where to go, but I *damn* sure knew I didn't want my Kaleb forgotten. So, I set out to figure out this "healing," only to realize I had to figure out that there *is* no healing. It is instead about learning how to love life and rebuild it around your loss, which I have done and continue to do daily. I was a hot mess in my journey, not going to lie; but my hope is to help you ladies down your path, and in the journey you will now travel.

Ladies, I write this book for *you*. It is very raw, and I hold nothing back. Nothing was left out of what I experienced and what I have thought from the beginning to the present day. I've included everything in hopes that if you have felt at least one of my thoughts or feelings, you know you are not alone.

As I sit and write these words, it is my 10th Mother's Day without my child. Guess what? Today I cried thinking about my Kaleb. I tell you this to let you know that even 11 years later, I still cry—I still think of him, and I still talk about him. It's just what we do and it's completely normal. I give you permission to be emotional, but what I *don't* give you permission to do is to live your life in your emotion. Go ahead, read that again!

This book was written for you Mommas, of course, but I write it to help family and friends who don't understand what you are going through but want to help. All I can do is write from a momma's eyes, and that is why this book is for you. It may help men and women going through other types of loss, but my experience is jaded to child loss.

Life as you knew it has forever changed. Morals and values you once believed are now just memories of who you were. There is no going back to your former self, and I hate to be the one that has to break this to you. You will lose friends and family; you will gain new friends and some you may even consider family—it is all part of this new journey you will travel. As you begin this process, rebuild a life that your angel child would be proud of. It doesn't matter who you were or where you were before your child loss. If you take the opportunity to find out who you are after your child loss, this is a new beginning.

There is no good way to talk about child loss. This is exactly why everyone is uncomfortable speaking about children dying. It's why we feel silenced and lonely. There is a disclaimer: In this book, I will talk about things that may upset you, may make you angry, or even make you throw this book across the room. Learn to deal with it, because we *have* to talk about all of it—even the parts you hide from the world to see. I will take you through my whole story and what I learned in order to transform my life. Each chapter shares a step that you will need to walk on your own. They will each give you guidance on what has worked for me, and therefore a starting point on things you can try to help you.

I hope this book starts a new chapter in your life. One where you know that there are millions of mommas with angel babies. My wish is that you make the choice today to live life to its fullest, while still honoring your angel.

Maybe you found this book yourself or maybe it was given to you by someone else. Either way, I am honored you picked it up and proud of you for reading thus far. With that being said: Let's begin.

You can do the impossible because you have been through the unimaginable.

–Christina Rasmussen

Chapter 1:

The Nightmare Begins

I am not a movie star, nor a famous singer or influencer. I am just a momma to two of the most amazing children. Of course, I am biased, but they have taught me more about how beautiful life truly is than anyone.

Never would I believe my life would be anything more than being a momma working a nine-to-five, and I was okay with that; I don't need much. I love being a momma, and although until I was 28 I thought I would NEVER have kids, I look back at myself during that time and laugh. Boy was I so confused and such a spoiled brat.

My life was forever changed the day my Kaleb was born and the day he gained his angel wings. Until that day, I lived a life of confusion and a life I thought was my destined path. I had my Kaleb, my military husband, my favorite furbaby Katie, and a house on 5 acres in the country. What I would learn is my life was about to be flipped upside down when Kaleb was born, and then again when he died.

With that being said, here is my story.

My Story

I truly didn't believe I would ever have kids; I am just going to throw that one out there again. I never believed that raising children was the thing for me, but this all changed when I was 28 years old and my grandfather "Pap" died. When Pap died, I began thinking about my parents not being grandparents to *my* kids one day. If I was going to have kids, now was the time I really needed to start thinking about it. And in my mind, I decided in that short time that I would have a child and as soon as possible. Seriously, just like that, the girl who never was going to have a child decided she would—and fast! I will say, today I think about life decisions more than I did at 28.

Fast-forward to Thanksgiving Eve on November 25, 2009, at 10 p.m. My husband and I were rushing to the emergency room because, at the time, I thought I was having my Kaleb 5 weeks early. For both of us it was our first child, and we did not know what to expect. I called my mom and told her that we were heading to the hospital, and remember asking her if there was a lot of blood when her water broke. She told me there was some, but I thought nothing of it. Just for reference, there was so much blood I had to wrap a towel around me like a diaper.

When we arrived at the emergency room, we told the staff I was bleeding. I guess they thought it was normal too, because we sat for over an hour before they took us back. It seemed everyone was thinking about Thanksgiving the next day, not work.

When we were finally taken back, I was thrown a gown and told to put it on and lay on the bed. As I was trying to put it on, blood was running down my legs and I asked my husband to help me wipe it off. I guess we were taking too long, and the nurse opened the door. When she saw blood running down my legs and the pool that collected on the floor, she told me just to get on the bed. After I got back on the bed, everything started to move so fast. The nurse was pressing buttons like she was chasing down stars in the original Mario Bros. Suddenly the door busted open and there was a doctor, telling me to get on my knees on the bed so they could try and find my Kaleb's heartbeat. I was advised to lie back on the bed, and the doctor told me I needed a C-section to deliver my Kaleb. I was in so much pain that I told her to just do what she had to do. The medical staff told my husband to kiss me goodbye, and I was rolled through the doors to surgery. I can remember them taking off my earrings, ring, and necklace while I was being rolled down the hall. I wasn't scared or anxious at the time, I was just hurting. I remember being told to breathe deep and I did as soon as he told me—then I was out.

I don't remember when it was, but I eventually woke up and saw white, bright lights. It was like I couldn't see anything but light, and I desperately asked, "Is he alive?" Someone said, "They are working on him." I asked again, "Is he alive?!" And I was told again, "They are working on him." To this day, I don't know who I was speaking with.

By the time I woke up again, I was in a room with my mom and my little brother. While I was sleeping, there was so much going on that I am glad I missed it. I learned I had a complete placental abruption and had lost 3 1/2 pints of blood. Kaleb was not breathing when he was born and the wonderful Dr. Robert Criscuola (Doc) kept working on him until he started breathing. Years later, I asked Doc why he worked so hard on Kaleb. Doc said babies just tell you and Kaleb wanted to live. It was decided by Doc to put Kaleb on a cooling blanket (he had to be on this at least six hours after he was born), but this required him to be transported to a hospital in Atlanta, Georgia. And with the weather being foggy, a flight was out of the question. So, Kaleb was rushed out of the hospital into an ambulance and driven to Grady Memorial Hospital in Atlanta, Georgia, which was four hours away. My dad and my husband, Brian, followed the ambulance to Grady. By the grace of only God, Kaleb made it on the cooling blanket within six hours and everyone arrived alive. I don't even want to know how wild that ride was!

My mom, my little brother Todd, my bestie, Jen, and friend Ashlee were all in the hospital just sitting and waiting. I never got to see Kaleb, but one of the nurses took pictures of him and printed them out for me. He was absolutely gorgeous and perfect.

Being Thanksgiving, the dinner my big brother Scot, Todd, and my mom had consisted of McDonald's hamburgers and fries. Happy Thanksgiving, right?! I believe after learning the series of events that had taken place, we all were the most Thankful we had ever been. Both Kaleb and I were alive, and we were together.

I would remain in the hospital for a few days, as I had lost so much blood. My skin was yellow (olive skin peeps will understand this) and I was so weak. After I managed to eat a roll and some crackers, I was finally released to go home, but I was in so much pain. I was given some iron pills and told to rest and make all my follow-up appointments. Rest was far from what I did, though. The next day, on November 29th, my mom and I headed to Grady's NICU to see my

Kaleb, Brian, and my dad. Remember to this point, I had not seen my Kaleb in person.

I could write a whole book on the experience in the NICU; but in short, Grady's NICU is amazing. And I finally got to hold my Kaleb for the first time on December 6th. After everything I had just experienced, it was heavenly, and we would be connected every day after. My husband and I would spend every day in the NICU, all day, until they made us go home for the night. Home became a Best Western hotel room for a few hours a night. We would be back when they would allow us every morning. After spending three and a half weeks at Grady, we were able to leave. I can't remember if we came home on Brian's birthday, December 23rd (which was Kaleb's due date), or on December 24th. Either way, we were home for Kaleb's first Christmas, and it was perfect. My parents ran out to buy a Christmas tree and put it up. It was one of the most thankful and emotional Christmases I've ever experienced. We were just so happy to be together in our little world with our little family.

With the trauma of Kaleb's birth, he had a lack of oxygen to his brain. This caused several issues that the cooling blanket could not fix. Kaleb would have a seizure disorder, cerebral palsy, microcephaly, and cortical blindness to name a few. This did not matter to us though: He was our perfect boy and we had both survived. I can remember telling Kaleb many times, "We are in this together." Because that is what I thought—we both lived for each other.

We were now parents to a special needs child. It was a different life— not only were we new parents but Kaleb could not feed himself, he wasn't mobile, and he had more doctors than I could count on one hand. He had physical therapy, occupational therapy, speech therapy, and eye therapy. He saw a team of doctors every three and a half months at Shands Children's Hospital in Gainesville Florida—Go Gators.

I could write an entire book on being the parent of a special needs child. There are so many trials and tribulations. There are so many ups and downs we experienced, but we always somehow made it work. We believed we had made it through, and just needed to get into a routine and give Kaleb what he needed. It was no longer about us as a couple;

it was what Kaleb needed and we both were completely committed to his health and well-being. Remember I told you earlier that Kaleb and I were in it together, our worst times were past us—until I woke up to Brian screaming on March 20, 2012.

March 19th had been a pretty normal day. I went to work and if I remember correctly, Brian and Kaleb took the day off to go to Kaleb's doctor appointments at Shands. They were gone all day and were heading back in the late afternoon. My mom had called and said she'd messed up the TV remote and asked if I would come by and fix it. Messing up the DISH remote, as I am writing this book, still happens often. I told her I would stop by on my way home. At the same time I was going home, Brian and Kaleb were on their way home. I told Brian to stop by my mom and dad's house too. Of course, he did, and they got to see Kaleb. The remote was fixed, and we all sat and talked for a little while before heading home. Home was a quarter of a mile behind my parents, so not a long distance at all. As we made it home, Kaleb was tired from the day because he fell asleep pretty fast.

Brian and I were on a routine. Kaleb would wake up several times in the middle of the night and we would switch waking up to comfort him and change out his feeding tube bag. At 4 a.m. on March 20, 2012, I woke up to Brian screaming. I can remember jumping out of bed and running down the stairs asking him what was wrong. He said that Kaleb wasn't breathing, and I don't know why but I asked him if he was joking. He was crying and screaming, "No!" I ran down the rest of the stairs, into the kitchen, and dialed 911. I threw down the phone and ran into Kaleb's room. A back story on where we live—if someone dials 911 and no one answers, the police have to respond anyway. When I made it to Kaleb's room, Brian was performing CPR on Kaleb on the bed. I told him to go talk to the police, moved Kaleb to the floor, and began performing CPR on him. We both knew CPR because we had to become certified before we left the hospital, and we both had to be certified because he was in the military, and I was in law enforcement. I could hear Brian talking to dispatch and he came and brought me the phone. I started talking to them, and even though I knew the entire dispatch crew from working with them for so long, I couldn't tell you who I was talking to. I was telling them that he didn't have a pulse and I was doing compressions. Between answering questions, I would talk to Kaleb, telling him to come on and *breathe.* I remember yelling at Brian to call my dad. I don't know how long I was performing CPR before I saw two Paramedics (EMTs) come into Kaleb's room. I handed Kaleb to them, and they ran out of the house.

I then left Kaleb's room and started getting all of his medications together for EMS and the hospital. In a rush, I grabbed them and passed my dad, who had made it to our house. He looked at me and asked what was wrong. I looked at my dad and said, "Everything is going to be okay." As I opened the front door, my front yard was filled with a sea of blue and red lights. There were deputy cars and ambulances everywhere. I ran to the ambulance Kaleb was in and handed them the medication, before stepping back and allowing them to take Kaleb away. Still to this day, I have no idea how I was able to remain so calm. I truly believe it was my law enforcement training, and when the trauma started, I kicked into a different mode—just like I had done in situations as a law enforcement officer. I believe being a law enforcement officer was a good thing and a bad thing. I knew what to do, but I was also privy to the way things are worded when a situation is not good.

As Brian and I were getting ready to leave. One of the officers I knew well came up to me and said we had to wait on Alicia, who was an investigator I knew. We both looked at each other in silence. I knew and he knew, but my dad and Brian did not. I told my dad we had to wait on the investigator and told him to head to the hospital.

I walked out back, and the deputy walked outside with me. I knew... I knew because I had myself been in the same situations with families. In our county, whenever a child died an investigator would be sent out to speak with the parents and look around the house—just in case there was foul play in the child's death. My Kaleb was dead, and the officer and I were the only ones who knew. I walked to the back porch and leaned on it while the officer made small talk with me. We briefly spoke about what we both already knew. He asked if I wanted to write a note that he and the other deputies could stay and wait for Alicia to arrive and do the investigation. The note was written, and Brian and I headed to the hospital, leaving our house to the deputies.

On the way to the hospital, it was pretty quiet in the car. Brian wanted me to drive faster, but I kept telling him we needed to be safe and there was no point in going fast. In my mind, I didn't want to get to the hospital. I felt the slower I was going, the longer I could prolong Brian knowing. I finally got up enough courage (I guess you could say) and told him, "You know, when we get to the hospital, it might not be good." I can't remember exactly what he said in return, but it was something about not being negative and to think positive. I didn't say anything else. I just sat with my thoughts, trying to make the drive longer in order to prolong what I knew we were going to be told at the hospital.

I had so many thoughts running through my head. How was I going to "fix" this? Being in law enforcement, I always wanted to fix the situation and make it better. I was trying to make his death be okay in my mind. I thought to myself, *Well at least he's not hurting anymore. Right?* That was a positive, but no matter how I looked at it, my Kaleb was gone. What was I going to do now? My life was consumed by my baby boy. Everything I did on a daily basis was all about my Kaleb. Even at the beginning of my loss journey, my mind could not see the future without him in it. What the hell was I supposed to *do* now? Then, my mind brought me back to the current situation at hand. Brian who was sitting beside me, not even knowing the severity of the situation yet. My parents maybe, because they had beat us to the hospital—but not Brian. I can remember thinking, *This is not going to be good. How the heck are we going to deal with this?*

When we got to the hospital we jumped out of the car and, holding hands, ran to the front desk. We told the clerk that our son was brought in and then I heard my name, "June." I turned to see another officer I had worked with. He was working extra duty at the hospital. I explained to him what was going on and he shuffled us to a private waiting room. He knew too. Brian and I sat there until the doctor and a chaplain came in. And then, what I knew was coming happened. Words no parent ever wants to hear... "I'm sorry, we did everything we could, but your son has passed away." Brian lost it and started crying. I looked at the ground, still trying to be strong. I put my hand over my eyes, fighting back the tears. I felt like I had to be strong and stoic still. Then they told us they would take us to our son.

As we walked down the hall and turned down the corner, I could see my parents standing outside a room door. My parents were crying and when I got to them, I just lost it. I sat down on the ground, covered my face in between my knees, and started sobbing. And there I stayed. I don't know if someone helped me get up or I got up myself, but eventually I stood and walked into his room. I grabbed his lifeless body and held him, rocking back and forth saying, "My baby, my baby boy." I didn't want to let him go. In what felt like a minute, the chaplain was telling me it was time to go. I hugged him and kissed him one last time. It was the last time that I would ever see my son. My nightmare had begun, just like that. Later, I would realize, it was the first day of Spring the day Kaleb died.

I remember setting my Kaleb back down on the bed, but I don't remember leaving the room. I remember walking out to the main lobby and seeing my coworker Will. I had accidentally called him instead of my boss on the way to the hospital. I can't tell you what we talked about, though. I don't remember getting back into the vehicle to leave the hospital or even the drive home. I remember turning alarms off on my phone—alarms I had set for Kaleb's medication doses and my time to wake up for work. I have no idea why of all things, I remember that. I also remember just the shock, like I was in a dream. Some call it a fog, like… *Did this really just happen? Am I dreaming?* Maybe at first that's why—when I was performing CPR on my child, when I was driving to the hospital, when we were with the chaplain—I was "strong." I had no emotion, like my mind was trying to process everything while simultaneously just going through the motions. The only way I can describe it is pure and utter shock. Just completely numb, as I tried to process the enormity of what had just happened. I now have many years behind me to realize my mind was trying to catch up with the sequence of events that happened within a four-hour window.

This is my story. I am one of many of us out there who are trying to deal with our child's loss. Your story is not my story but what I have found is, sometimes listening to someone else's story helps us realize just how similar we are. Obviously, my child died when he was two years old and for some of you, your child lived to be an adult and had babies of their own. It's not about what stage our children were at in life or how they passed—we all are one. We might not understand each other's story, but we *do* understand the pain. With each of us who go through the loss of a child, we understand what worked for us may work for others who are dealing with child loss.

I recently was speaking with a momma who stated that she did not want to talk about her child loss because people would never understand. She was in the beginning stages of her child loss, and I totally get it. What she did not understand is that telling her story will help her come to terms with her child loss. It will help her realize she is not alone. Remember this: We all need to know we are not alone, and we need to know that what we are feeling isn't as crazy as we think. Later in the book, I will get into more detail about this—but each time you tell your story, it gets easier. It helps you realize that no matter how much time has passed, your child is not forgotten and will always be remembered.

When you are in your beginning stages of grief, try to be open to telling your story. Keep your mind and eyes open to new experiences and those around you who can help you. In the beginning, we think we are alone; but what we learn after our child loss is just how many mommas are experiencing the same. Mommas who have lost a child will be your biggest cheerleaders. They will be there for you when you think no one else will be.

As this first chapter comes to a close, I want you to take away a few things from it. I hope you have realized that you are far from being alone. There are so many of us out here—in every state and in every country. We are united as one, and we have experienced—or are experiencing—something that most will never go through or possibly understand. Be open to new experiences and be willing to accept possibilities for help. Realize if you try it and don't like it, you don't have to do it again. You are the one steering the wheel. Your journey is now in your hands. Where you go and what impact you will have on the world is up to you. Live a life that your child would be proud of. If you can't do it for you right now, do it for *them*. You got this, Momma!

And then all the sudden she changed. She came back a completely different person: with a new mindset, a new outlook, a new soul.

The girl that once cared way too much about everybody and everything, no longer cared at all.

–Laurelin Paige

Chapter 2:

My Child Died: Now What?

As we left the hospital after learning of Kaleb's death, I don't remember if we said anything or if it was a silent ride home. I know I was in pure shock—was this really happening to me right now? Like many of you, I was thinking it had to be a bad dream and I was going to wake up any second and realize it was not my new reality. Eleven years later, and I still haven't woken up; unfortunately, it wasn't a dream—it's a reality I had to face.

When we made it home, it was light outside. We walked inside to silence. I went to Kaleb's room to clean up the milk that had spilled from unhooking his feeding tube when the paramedics took him out of the room. I hadn't thought to turn it off, so it kept pumping his food onto the floor until the bag ran out. The machine was beeping, telling us that we needed to add more food—but of course, we hadn't been home. As I think back now, I have no idea why, after I got home, that was the most important thing. Who wants to clean up a mess in that situation? But now that I look back at it, I think that I knew it was the last time something like that would happen. Maybe it was giving my mind something else to think about, besides him passing away and the sequence of events that just took place. I don't really know, but I remember that was the most important thing on my mind at the time.

After I cleaned the milk up, I went outside and sat in a chair, staring out at the hayfield in front of my house. I remember just staring and playing everything over in my head again. I was in shock, and I just did not even know what to think. Numbness had consumed me—holy crap, what was going on?! My gosh, did this just happen? *Am I dreaming?*

Losing a child is a huge shock—and remember, when all of this happens, our mind is not sure how to react. Our mind knows that it is an event, that there needs to be a feeling assigned to it and it is trying to figure out what to feel. In the first moments, weeks, and months into your child loss, don't evaluate how you reacted. I have spoken with mommas who have so much guilt wrapped around the fact that they didn't cry, or they didn't do a particular thing, right at the moment they found out. They feel guilty, they feel horrible, that they did not react a certain way. They feel they did not love their child enough or they weren't a good mom. Momma, your mind is trying to process everything that is going on. Don't think not crying or being emotional has anything to do with the love for your child or the kind of mother you were. It is just a reaction, and nothing more.

As I was sitting in that chair outside, something happened. At first, I did not think much about it—but now, I think it was a sign. Now I am traditionally not an, "It's a sign," kind of person; but for Kaleb and my brain to process, it was a sign. When I looked to my right, by a tree, there was a deer. It had walked out of the field and was standing in my front yard, staring at me. I stared back at it, and we just kept eye contact for what seemed like an eternity; then it walked across my yard and into the woods that surrounded my house. Now that I look back at that moment, I feel it was a sign—a sign from Kaleb that he was okay and that I was going to be okay.

Many people had learned of Kaleb's death. Remember, I was in law enforcement and knew all the officers at my house and at the hospital. No one knows what to do when a child dies, so they come to visit and bring food. I remember the kitchen was full of food—on the counters, on the tables... so much we had to bring another table in to accommodate more food. Did I mention, I wasn't eating at the time? I wanted *nothing* to do with food. I just wanted to sit and stare. My mind could not process what was going on, or who was at my house. I couldn't remember who came to visit but I was trying to remember to thank them later; but the later never happened because I couldn't remember.

My mind was all over the place during the first few days, but I felt I needed to be brave. I needed to not cry in front of anyone. In doing this, I denied myself time to grieve; I felt like I had to hide and be "strong" like everyone thought I was. But I wasn't strong. I was a hot mess, and I was devastated.

My crying and grieving were done in the shower and behind closed doors, where no one could see me. Everyone had to know though, my eyes were bloodshot from lack of sleep and crying. I would cry until I could not cry anymore. Momma, if I can tell you anything, it is to cry and grieve *openly*. No one is judging you; no one is thinking anything less of you, and no one is worrying about anything but you. It is okay to release every bit of the tears you have for your child. Don't feel obligated to hide and feel your true emotions alone—because when you do, this is where the loneliness starts. This is where our mindset starts to change, and we start to believe we are alone. I am not saying Loudmouth Linda from down the street, who came to be nosy is the person you want to release all of your emotion on—but I think you get the point. Find your people and be open with them. Your people will protect you and keep your daily life moving in the beginning days, when you can't seem to move yourself.

On the first day (and following days) before the funeral, loved ones (especially if you live in a small town like I do) will try to help and support you in the best way they know how, since they really just don't know what to do. If you are like me, you just want to hide and be alone—and that is okay. Momma, in the first days when you are trying to process your grief, if you want to be alone and by yourself, honor that need. You do not have to be polite; you do not have to greet anyone who comes to your house. Have a family member do that—or if you don't want them in your house, have a family member greet them at the front door. This is not being rude and please don't apologize for anything! You are still processing everything that has just happened; it is okay. It is not your obligation to be Momma right now.

The first days those individuals came over, I felt obligated to sit with them. I would sit gazing off, not really thinking about anything. I felt obligated to make sure everyone that came saw me, and I thanked them for coming and let them give me their condolences. I thought that was what I *had* to do—but within two days, I couldn't do it anymore. I remember talking to one of my dad's coworkers, James, on the phone. My dad had told him I was not eating, and he asked me if I would eat a cheese pizza if he brought it to me. I said yes, knowing I wouldn't but wanting to accept James' sincere gesture.

James and his wife ended up coming over to the house to see me, but I was at the point where I came out of my room and thanked him without going downstairs. I just couldn't do it anymore. My Aunt Kay and Uncle Roy came over, but I still just couldn't anymore. More people came over and I just laid in my bed crying with my furbaby Katie or watching TV. Brian would come up and tell me who was there and ask if I would come down. I always sent him away by telling him "No." I did not want to go downstairs.

I was done, and we hadn't even planned Kaleb's funeral yet because we were still waiting on his body to come back from the Georgia Bureau of Investigation's crime lab. Yes, I said that right: the crime lab. In the State of Georgia, any unexpected child death results in the child being sent to the crime lab for an autopsy in order to make sure there was no foul play involved. And guess what? I knew the crime lab employees too. I remember Rodney calling me still to this day. He told me he was sorry about Kaleb and that they were going to do the autopsy as soon as they received him. Rodney told me they weren't going to do a full autopsy because of his medical history, but I remember telling Rodney to please try and find out what happened. I wanted to know what happened: Why now? What had stopped working?

As a momma, I understood that my son died—but it had already started to bother me as to *why* he died. Why did he stop breathing *now*? Did his heart stop, did his brain stop sending vital signals to his body, did his organs shut down? Why now?! He was finally on the right medications—we gave him his medications on time every day, we fed him his food through a pump when he needed it, and we took him to all his doctor's appointments. He was just at his doctor's appointments, and he was fine. I needed to know why. I had to know what I could have done differently—because it had to be my fault, right? Ahh Mommas, do you see me already telling myself stuff that was just not true? Do you see where I am already telling myself that I did something wrong? There will be more on that later!

The autopsy came back and there was no underlining factor that would lead the crime lab to believe it was one thing over another. They could not pinpoint anything other than Kaleb's death was the cause of the trauma his body experienced when he was born. His body could not hold on any longer. I would never know what exactly stopped first, and I would never know why I lost my Kaleb—and that was a tough truth to swallow.

Mommas, if you are in my position, it can be a rough one. Not knowing exactly how your child died or what happened can lead your mind to meander more than you can imagine. Does it really matter, though? After everything you have just gone through, does it matter? At the time, it may feel that it is the most important thing, like it did with me—but please know it's not. We have to learn to accept that we may never know and unfortunately, we have to learn to be okay with that. I know that may not be what you want to hear, but that is me keeping it real with you.

For all of you Mommas who struggle with knowing the cause of your child passing, you will face much uncertainty. Your struggle is in the form of questioning what you could have done differently to stop your child's death. The truth is, if you allow yourself to, you will live the rest of your life mulling over the what ifs and should haves. It will eat at you and will some days drive you mad. Acknowledge the "how," and accept that you cannot change the outcome. Live in the now and stop beating yourself up, Momma.

I could have opened a Hallmark store with the number of cards that we were getting in the mail. The cards poured in from all over the United States, from people we did not even know... people who saw our story and just wanted to tell us how sorry they were. Individuals in your life—and church organizations or even 501(c)(3) organizations—may reach out to you. Be open to their help and guidance. Write down their website and their number, just in case one day you want help. I will say this, Momma—do not jump into anything new at the beginning stages of your grief.

I joke a lot about all the food and the cards that came in at the time of Kaleb's death. But at a time when our house felt so empty and our hearts were breaking, it meant the world to us. I wish I could thank all of the individuals who took the time to care when we were going through the worst time of our lives, but I can't—nor could I remember everyone.

I also warn you about the medication that they may wish to put you on—this elephant in the room needs to be talked about briefly. There is a stigma with medication that individuals are placed on when their child dies. What you choose to do is your choice, and your choice alone. My advice—I urge you to be mindful of how much medication they put you on in the beginning. There are a few reasons why I say this.

First, I have seen mommas who are placed on so much medication that they can barely function in society. In my personal opinion, the dosage of the medication these mommas were on would not allow them to grieve, much less do anything but sit and sleep. Seek a professional, but not *just* a professional—a professional who has helped other mommas navigate child loss. Someone who can at least relate. Second, I urge you to think about the medication and your life. Is it a good fit for you? When we lose a child, medication is a top priority with some doctors. If medication is mentioned to you, accept that you can get it if you need it, go home and think about it, and try to do without it for a few days. If you find you need it, then get the medication. In the world we live in today, everything is habit-forming. I can name a few things I am addicted to on one hand. Be careful and have a game plan ready. The most important thing I can tell you, Momma, is you know *you*—you know what you will need. Your life is turned upside down right now; but deep down, you will know what is best for you. For me, I chose not to take medication.

If you are struggling with your child loss, don't wait to get help. Sometimes there is a stigma behind therapy, and Momma, throw that idea out the window right now. Stop deciding that therapy is not for you or that no one can help you before you even try it. What is the worst that can happen? You don't like therapy and you don't go back? Just like with the medication, I feel you need the right professional to help you with your loss. You need to find that person who you mesh well with. I know we don't like talking to strangers about our loss, but I also know you have met those people in your life who, the first time you spoke, you just knew that they were *your* people. It breaks my heart to watch mommas struggle by themselves because they feel therapy is not going to work for them. It is not good for you, and you don't deserve to be in this alone.

There are alternatives to therapy—we have support groups, and there are tons of Facebook groups. They are not all created equal though, Mommas. Be picky about where you spend your time and be picky about the types of conversations in these groups. Is it always negative? Are they trying to truly help you or are they a bunch of individuals who are always negative?

When I began my child loss journey, I did not have a support group which focused just on child loss in my area. There was instead a support group for everyone who had lost someone special to them. I am not saying that these groups cannot help you, but sometimes these groups make us feel even more alienated. Sometimes with mixed groups, we will feel like a small population; but in reality, there are millions of us scattered throughout the world.

I have joined many Facebook groups more recently—in fact, I've joined them and unjoined them. The problem I have with a lot of these groups is, they allow you to talk about child loss, but they don't try and help you move forward in your loss. So, you get a bunch of individuals posting about how they will never get over their loss. They post how they are 5 to 10 years in, and it still hurts like the day that they lost their child. This is not good, Mommas! The new mommas who are coming into these groups are seeing these posts, which they will eventually post themselves, and in the process change their mindset without even knowing it. They are reading that you never get over it, so they believe *they* will never get over their child loss. They see this message so much in these groups that their new belief becomes, *I will never get over the loss of my child, how could I if Linda is 10 years in, and she didn't get over it?* Wrong answer, Momma! You are closing your mind to the possibility that you can rebuild your life and enjoy life again. Seek groups that encourage remembrance and encourage growth. These are the groups that will allow you to lovingly remember your child, help you on your hard days, and encourage you to grow into the new life that you will make for yourself.

The Funeral

I was not prepared for the funeral—I don't believe that anyone could be. Just days into my loss, I had to start making decisions for Kaleb's funeral. I can remember going to McLane Funeral Home; and of course, they were as nice as could be. There are no words to describe talking to a funeral home about your two-year-old's funeral. How do you make the last decisions you will make for your child in a few hours? How do you take a lifetime they were supposed to spend with you and end it in one final farewell?

Of everything we had to do, looking at the caskets and deciding what his burial site would look like was the absolute hardest. I knew I wanted Kaleb in a suit with his glasses, and I knew I wanted him buried—but everything else, I just did not know. We picked out the songs they would sing, the programs they would use... everything had to be perfect—even the little casket they would carry his body in. The casket was silver—it was beautiful, and it was perfect, just like Kaleb was to us. He would have this big arch and a huge stone and a little bench to sit on when I came to visit him. The grass would be taken out of the family plots, and it would be replaced by rocks and granite markers, surrounding all of the family plots. He would be buried by my grandparents and my great-grandparents. It was everything I could have imagined it would be—and more. I was not going to change my mind; it was exactly what I wanted. While they were totaling the amount, my mom made the comment (I can't remember the exact words), "This seems expensive, do you want to check some other prices?" I looked at my mom and told her, "This is the last thing I will ever buy Kaleb." With that, nothing more was said about it. Kaleb's funeral was expensive—hell, all funerals are expensive. By the way, if you are wondering, a child's funeral is exactly half the price of an adult's funeral. And if I had to do it all over again, I would spend the same amount.

Momma, I tell you this story to tell you this: Do what is going to make you happy and do what is going to put you at peace. We often face so many struggles when trying to find peace, don't let this be one of them. You are going to have those who may question what you are doing—they may even say something about it. They mean absolutely no harm by it, but you will need the voice of reason in your life at this time. In the end, do what is going to make you happy and spare no expense. As hard as it was for me to do this in my journey, I am so glad I did.

The night before Kaleb's funeral, we got all dressed up and headed to the funeral home before anyone else was to arrive. I remember standing at the back of the room, not wanting to go into where Kaleb was. We had videos displaying pictures of Kaleb, we had still pictures on easels, and there were flowers everywhere from families I knew and some I did not. It was beautiful, just like he was.

I personally knew I did not want to see Kaleb in his casket. I knew it was beautiful and my mom and dad said he looked great, but nope—did want to see him. They tried to urge me to go and see him one last time, but I was not doing it. I already had the image of him lying on the hospital bed burnt into my memory, and I did not want another image to go along with it. I kindly declined and kept toward the back of the room. Everyone was coming and going—it was so packed, there were so many people there.

As I scanned the room I saw Doc, the man who saved his life two years earlier during his birth. The man that I owed so much to, even at a time when I was so hurt and so emotional. Doc understood—no, he never had lost a child, but he was there from day one and knew everything that Kaleb had gone through. He knew how special Kaleb was and how much of a fighter he was. As soon as I saw him, I walked over to him, he asked me if I was alright, and I said, "No." Until this point, I was strong, I was holding it together—but as I hugged Doc I just began to cry. Every bit of emotion came pouring out to Doc. I still to this day don't know what he or his wife, Christine, were thinking—but I felt safe. I felt safe to feel and to not be judged. After I finally let go, I went outside and sat on a bench, just letting people come and go, simply passing time. My cousin, Jonathan (another doctor) came and sat next to me. I can't remember what he said but I replied, "It just sucks." Jonathan is not at all a funeral kind of guy and him being there meant a lot. He said something to me that day that I still remember. He said, "No parent should have to go through this, it's just not fair."

Jonathan was right. No parent should have to go through child loss. It is the most unimaginable roller coaster. For this reason and this reason alone, we carry a scarlet letter across our forehead, not even our chest. You know what? Wear that scarlet letter with pride, Mommas. If anyone ever makes you feel like anything less than a grieving parent, say goodbye to them and move on. Don't waste your time and energy on them. As days go by, you are going to remember times like these in your child loss, when someone touches you with little acts of kindness. Both Doc and Jonathan never experienced child loss like I have, but it was the few words they spoke to me that meant so much. Still to this day, I believe they came expecting they could do nothing for me but gave me their whole heart anyway—the only thing they could possibly do for me in that moment.

The day of the funeral, the 25th, was kind of the same as the night before—except it was pouring. I found out later it was National Cerebral Palsy Awareness Day. It was fitting for the day, and it rained long and hard. I tried to be stoic and strong and did good until just about the end when "Tears In Heaven," by Eric Clapton, broke me. I was done. I cried and cried and cried, walking out to the vehicle that would take us to the cemetery. On the drive to the gravesite, it stopped raining and the sun began to shine. We had set a bunch of roses in buckets for those who came to the ceremony and they put roses on the casket after they came up to greet us. I am sure there was a lot going on at the gravesite but, to tell you the truth, I don't remember. I do remember his daycare, Pediatria, wanting to release balloons into the air. As the balloons were released, they scattered throughout the sky but then came together and rose until we could see them no more.

And that was the end. That was the last time I had to plan and organize anything that big for my son. It was the last time I would have so many people together honoring the life of my son. I could not fathom, my Kaleb, not being remembered. Even at this point in my journey I knew I would not be okay and could not live if this was it. My life had forever changed, but I had to find a way to keep Kaleb close to me.

One of the biggest fears I hear from mommas is that their child will be forgotten. That over time, people will not remember. This is the furthest from the truth—they will remember that your child lived, they will remember who they were, and they will remember who you were before your child passed. It is our responsibility to tell our story and to shout their names. You are the key to keeping your child's memory alive. It's on you, Momma, and I know you are up for the challenge.

When the funeral and all the planning are done, and when the last people are gone, it goes back to quiet. You have nothing left to do for your child. Now you feel that it is time to "heal" or "move on," or whatever notions people have placed in your head. I think you know, Momma, there is no moving on from child loss. After the funeral is over, I want you to stop thinking that it is the end—because it is not. It is the end of your child passing, but it is the beginning of their *legacy*. Their legacy lives on within you and will never be forgotten, as long as you keep their fire burning.

Say it with me, Momma: "Your child's passing is over, but your child's legacy now begins." Now it's on you. You can choose to honor their life or hide them away. The obvious choice is to honor them. We all just have to get through the hard stuff first. It can be done, and is done by thousands of mommas each year. Make the choice right now. Put down this book, walk away to a quiet place, think about everything you have been through these past weeks or months, and decide today that your child is going to live on. You decide today, Momma, that you have a legacy to create for your beautiful angel.

Start over, my darling. Be brave enough to find the life you want and courageous enough to chase it. Then start over and love yourself the way you were always meant to.

–Madalyn Beck

Chapter 3:

Life Keeps Moving

All of the sudden, life has started to move forward. You aren't ready to move with it, but you have completed just about everything that needed to be done. You may or may not be back to work; but you know, you may need to think about working again. You are feeling lost right now and that is normal, Momma. As everyone continues with their daily life, you are still left to think about everything that seemed to happen only yesterday.

Are you noticing all the paperwork that has to be filled out and how much menial stuff has to be done after your child's death? I don't know where I heard this, but slow and steady wins the race. Don't think everything has to be done in a week or a day. If you have the time during your day, use it to get all the insurance paperwork done, copies of the death certificates, and all of the checks off to where they need to go for the funeral payments. These items will be extremely emotional for you, and they can drag on for what seems like months. I think the death certificates we had to get were the worst. Looking at the death certificate with the dates and times... It felt so final to me.

Unfortunately for me, I was in the last week of my last class writing my last paper I had procrastinated about for my bachelor's degree in Criminal and Social Justice. The timing could not be any worse, but I emailed my professor and secured an extension. Of course, my professor was understanding and gave me that extension—but not before I had to produce the program for my Kaleb's funeral. By this time, all I could think was, *Are you freaking kidding me? Who the hell would lie about their child's death?* I did what I was asked, and got the extension needed to finish my paper a week later and graduate. A time I thought would be one of my proudest moments turned into nothing more but a piece of paper that would come in the mail in five to seven business days.

Graduating with a bachelor's degree was going to be my second biggest accomplishment in my life, trampled by my first biggest accomplishment—my Kaleb. How ironic is that? After many years and a lot of living in my thoughts, I believe it was meant to happen just that way. First, in a twisted way, it reinforced how important family is to life. Second, it showed me that there is a lot more to life than a fancy degree or subsequent job I thought it would bring. Third, it gave me a glimpse of how a human can endure the impossible, be at the worst place in their life, and still rise to find strength they never believed they had. "You are stronger than you know," or "You are so strong." How many times have you heard this, Mommas? We learned to hate that phrase from those who don't understand what we are going through. Personally, every time I hear that phrase I think to myself, *Damn right I'm strong.* So, the next time you hear that phrase Momma, tell yourself, "Damn right I'm strong." Even if you don't believe it, think it and speak it until your mind agrees. *Yep, I am strong.*

After the first few weeks following Kaleb's death, I was ready to get back to work. At the time, I was working for a drug task force and there were only a few of us on the team. Almost every day after work, they would come to my house and sit with me. Most of the time they would joke and talk amongst themselves, but what they were talking about didn't really matter. It was just the fact they were there that meant so much. I knew that none of them understood, but it was good to see them and hear the crazy stories they would talk about and the day's events at work. We were all crazy and younger back then. Though I was ready to get back to work, my boss, Bahan, urged me to take the large amount of time off that I had. It's not that I loved work so much that I wanted to rush back or that I was finished grieving. It was instead a way to take my mind off of the current situation—my child loss.

When you are dealing with your child loss, I urge you to take the time that you need. There is a healthy amount of time to take off from work, and there is a healthy amount of time to wait before you go back. I chose the *unhealthy* time to go back. I went back way too early—so early, in fact, that I could have hurt myself or someone I cared deeply about.

In the first few weeks I was back at work, I was what I would call on light duty. I think everyone was still feeling me out, to see if I had enough of a level head to work. I guess I played it off really well, because I was going to participate in a search warrant of a residence where we were looking for drugs. They knew I didn't need to be on an entry team at least, and I was told to take the rear of a residence. I jumped out of the car and ran around the back of the house. As I made it to the back of the house, the door busted open, and people came running straight at me. I commanded them to get on the ground and they ran back inside. Then I heard a gunshot and ran around to the front of the residence to find everyone was okay. The gunshot I heard was a warning to a huge pit bull that had come out lunging at one of my partners. FYI—the dog did not die and lived a full life, don't worry. We did so much stuff in that house that day, searching and speaking to people. To this day, if I want to remember any of the details of this case, I will have to get the case file out and read it. I can't remember any of it. And guess what, Mommas, I went back to work way too early and made a risky choice that could have endangered everyone I went to that residence with.

In our grief, we still have to stay aware of our surroundings. Of course, you probably don't have the same job—I get it. But you may have a job where you could get someone hurt badly, or you could have a job where not putting data into the computer correctly could cause dire consequences and lose your company lots of business or money. My suggestion for all Mommas is to evaluate yourselves: Look at where you are when you are thinking of going back to work and ask yourself these questions:

- Do you have periods of time when you can really concentrate?

- Have you asked the therapist or medical professional you are seeing about going back to work? Do they feel you are ready?

- Why do you want to go back to work?

- Do you want to go back because you are tired of "feeling," or do you really feel in your heart it is time?

People go back to work for many reasons. When you are deciding if it is time or not, I want you to evaluate why (I know... to have to think in a time like this, right?!). I can tell you my reason—I wanted to stop sitting and doing nothing but thinking about Kaleb. I wanted to get out of the house and not see him in every single room I was in. I could not handle the loneliness, even when Brian would be sitting right next to me. I wanted to get back to some kind of normal and throw myself into work so I didn't have to feel what I was feeling anymore. I did not want to think about it, I did not want to cry about it. I just wanted to go back to the life I was living.

News flash, Mommas, this was about the unhealthiest thing I could have done. Instead of feeling those feelings and working through them, I pushed them to the back of my mind. You know the saying, "Out of sight, out of mind?" As long as I was working, I didn't have to deal with any of it. So I worked all day and all night, to the point where I came home exhausted. All I could do was fall asleep and wake up and do it all over again.

As much as it hurts, you have to allow yourself to *feel* all the emotions. You have to move through the emotions of your grief. Give yourself time to understand what has happened. Yes, you know your child died, but get an understanding and a grasp on life in your new journey. You don't have to figure out a timeline of set times and dates when you are going to feel emotions or when you are going to do specific things. Get an understanding that life is not going to be the same—understand there are upcoming challenges you may go through and get a grasp that in three weeks or 10 years, you still will have bad days. It's going to happen; you aren't immune to it. Just realize that this is an important part of rebuilding your life.

You could also not *want* to go back to work. I have seen mommas who don't have the urge to do anything, much less go back to work. I completely get that too! Some Mommas don't want to go back to the life they were living before their child loss. This signals the journey of living without your child, and it is unbearable right now. You may not want to deal with the alienation, the individuals wanting to talk to you about it, or to hear the work gossip that you are learning is not important at all. You have to start to get your life back eventually though, Momma. Don't hide from life, for you have done nothing wrong. Yes, you have lost a child—but your story is not over. Stop telling yourself you can't face the world and take baby steps toward it. It's not going to be easy at all, I am not going to lie to you about it; but the world is not asking you to be "fixed," it is asking you to join it again. What do you have to live for? You have so much—your other children, your husband, your parents, your pets, your friends. There is so much to live for, and people love you dearly.

You don't see it right now, Momma, but we are all here rooting for you. You can do this, I promise—and if you fall, there are a ton of us who will be here for you. If you have no one, then email me, find me on Facebook, write in the group, message me. We are in this together! Just like those who can't wait to get back to work, start thinking about *your* specific situation and ponder these questions:

- Why are you not wanting to go to work?

- Are you hiding from something?

- What do you feel is holding you back from getting back to work?

- What does your therapist or medical doctor say?

Look inside you and discover what it is. When you truly have an understanding about where you are, you can start the process of moving forward.

Like anyone who lost a child, I registered to begin my master's degree in Forensic Psychology a few months after I lost Kaleb (Joking: I just go with the decisions I made at this point in my loss). So, now on top of my work I was starting a master's degree—can you Mommas see the pattern? I was including things in my life which would keep me steady and busy. By doing this, I placed my grief files away to avoid dealing with them. During this time, I thought I could skid by the "healing process" that I was supposed to go through. You probably have guessed already; this is absolutely the *worst* thing you can do.

But I was the expert, right? I went to one therapy session, never to return. Plus, I already spoke with many individuals who never experienced child loss. They told me how to "heal" and how I would be just fine. I didn't need to read a damn book about grief or child loss—I was living the experience firsthand. Learning about another child's death would not help me. I was convinced of this.

Advice time, Momma. I just threw a lot out there, but there are two things I want you to remember. These are important, so highlight or dog-ear the page, or whatever you need to do.

First, you can't make the process go away by placing it in a file in the back of your mind. No matter how hard you try to push away the grief, the hurt, and the pain—it will still be there. You have to *go* through it, but in doing so you will find out more than you ever wanted to know about you as a person. I tried for many years to not think about my grief and totally not deal with it. I couldn't hide from it anymore when my daughter, Bella, was born—it came crashing down on me again. It is *good* to learn new things, take on projects, and decide to go back and get that degree that you never thought you would achieve. It's only *bad* if you don't give yourself the time daily to learn how to deal with your grief. If every day you come home from work, eat and go to sleep because you are exhausted from the day, only to get up and do it all over again—that's a clue you may be filing away your grief and not dealing with it. I wish I could tell you to do steps 1 through 10 and you will be cured. Because that's just it—there is no "cure." The cure is identifying and examining every single emotion you are going through. By doing this, you discover how your story, and your new life will coexist.

Second, it's okay to go to therapy and hear stories from other mommas who have lost children—and most importantly, it's okay *not* to be okay. Millions of women have gone through child loss, and what works for one momma may not work for another. That goes for anything in life. We try it and either like it and keep doing it, or we tweak it and see how we feel afterward. It is no different in a child's death. We listen to what has worked for some mommas (or the majority of them) and we try it. If it isn't a perfect fit for us, instead of throwing up our hands and saying, "This doesn't work for me," tweak it to fit your life. If this doesn't work, try something else. The key is to not stop and keep trying. *I know, June, but I don't want to keep trying, my child died.* Tough love moment: With that mindset, you are defeated before you even try.

You don't master something with one try. You may be good at something—but to truly master it, you must practice. You must have a positive mindset, and you have to have the *want*. Without this, you will stay in the same spot you initially started at. You can understand this with sports you may have played, the job you have now, or even in being married. These all take time to master, and we have to practice or repeat several times to master them. It works the same way with the trauma you are experiencing around your child's death.

I don't know who said this first about child loss but, "It's not a sprint, it's a marathon." We will deal with our child loss for the rest of our life. In a year, 5 years or 10 years, we will still be dealing with our child loss. Our life does not end the day our child died. We can choose to stay in the passenger seat, or we can live a life with purpose—one that our child or children will be proud of. Make the decision today that you will rise up from child loss and you will live a life honoring your angel.

Positive people are not positive because they've skated through life. They're positive because they've been through hell and decided they don't want to live there anymore.

–Mona Lisa Nyman

Chapter 4:

Who Has Time for Feeling?

So, you have buried your child, and you're still feeling numb and on autopilot—but now starts the feelings. This is the stuff people on the outside can only imagine you are going through, but your body is *screaming* for help. We don't have time for these feelings, because we're going through enough already. They come and they haunt you, though—even when you think they have passed, they come back again. It is normal, Mommas, and all part of the grief process.

When I was in the process of grieving, I had no clue where to start. I had gone through death before, but the closest death I had to deal with was my grandparents. Losing Kaleb was a dagger straight through my heart, and I couldn't imagine picking myself up and going on. That therapy session I went to? Yeah, it was no help—not that I would have really been listening, but they gave me nothing. I had no clue about grief in general and had no idea what to do. I was lost.

So years later, after my daughter Bella was born and I realized I might need to figure out how to "heal" while grieving, I started reading. Like everything I do, when I put my mind to it, I do it to the extreme. I read everything I could possibly think about reading. I obtained certificates in Neuro Linguistic Programming, Acceptance and Commitment Therapy, Cognitive Behavioral Therapy and Dialectical Behavioral Therapy. (I did say extreme). I listened to audiobooks one after the other and realized that there were other women who were thinking how I was thinking.

I am only guessing, but I am sure you don't know what good stuff to read or what to place your efforts into. If you were like I was, you don't even know the stages of grief. So, let's break this down a little because I believe having a foundation to start from is the best plan of action. Some feelings will not resonate with your individual experience, and some things will. The good part is that you will know what you are feeling is absolutely normal.

Elisabeth Kübler-Ross, if you don't know who she is, created the five stages of grief: denial, anger, bargaining, depression, and acceptance (Recover from Grief, 2020). I don't know who added two extra stages, but whoever it was, they were a genius because they got it correct. The seven stages of grief are defined as: shock and disbelief, denial, guilt, anger and bargaining, depression, loneliness and reflection, reconstruction, and acceptance. Okay, this is not a textbook and I refuse to bore you, but that is the foundation I want you to keep in the back of your mind. You may experience some of these emotions, or you may experience all of them. Some people feel this is an old-fashioned model of grief and to that I say: You are going to experience these emotions, so it's not so old-fashioned.

The Stages of Grief

Shock and Disbelief

Shock and disbelief are in the beginning. I know all of you have (or are) experienced it. Your mind just cannot comprehend exactly what happened. It's like a dream—a horrible dream you cannot wake up from. For moms who have children out of the home, those phone calls can be the most brutal ones. You are listening on the other line, but you are not comprehending what is being said after you heard your child has passed. This is followed up with wondering or asking, "Are you sure? This wouldn't happen to my child; I mean they were just here. They were doing better, and they were happy." Anything negative, and our mind will automatically try to switch the ending. It's as if our mind is trying to keep us from fully understanding what we are about to go through, and it's sometimes numbing.

I can remember being in so much shock that all I could do was sit. I couldn't cry, I couldn't eat, I couldn't speak... All I could do was stare and wonder what the hell just happened. If you are feeling any of these feelings, it is normal in the very beginning. For me, it lasted a week, maybe a little longer. I did start crying more after a few days, but my body was in so much shock I was just numb. If you haven't cried, if you just sat there and didn't know what to feel or do, that was normal. It was your mind and body trying to catch up with what just happened. For a while, I felt I was a horrible mother because I couldn't cry or process what was going on. Give yourself a break, Momma, it was (and is) a lot to process. If you have guilt, please don't give in to that ugly feeling. Know that the reactions you went through are okay, and let it go. Everyone feels differently in this moment even though it's solely shock and disbelief. There is no one way that you will go through this, and you might even skip this part completely. Thinking back now, can you recognize that you were in this stage?

Denial

Denial, yep, I felt that one too. Like I said, I felt like I was in a dream that I could not wake up from. I remember telling myself, "Are you kidding me? This isn't going on right now." I feel that even though denial goes together with shock and disbelief, it deserves its own stage. I know that denial came and went for me, as I am sure that it came and went for you. This stage is one that I don't believe you stay in long, but you can come back to it quickly.

My denial began as believing I was in nothing more than a dream. I could not make myself believe that I was childless and had to plan a funeral. I couldn't believe that I did not need to set an alarm to feed or give my child medication. For some Mommas, you may be in denial of an overdose, or possibly a number of possibilities you couldn't conceive your child of ever doing. They just weren't *raised* that way.

Touch love alert: No matter how we raise our children, they have their own mind and there are many things they will do—even when they know we would not agree with their decision. Whatever your circumstances are, Momma, you did experience child loss, it happened—I don't know why you have been chosen to go through this, but please know you are not alone. There are so many of us out here.

Guilt

Guilt—*oh* the guilt, Mommas. As many women who I have helped in the 11 years since my Kaleb passed, guilt is the one stage that many stay in—and some never get over this. Guilt can make you feel that as a Momma, you should have known that something was not right. But there are things that we just *don't know*. As much as we would like to think we could, sometimes that's just not the case. I don't know why as Mommas there are times, we have intuition and others we don't, but I will tell you—it does happen, and it has *nothing* to do with you as a Momma.

Another form of guilt I hear about is that momma who feels their child's deadly accident or sudden death has a direct link with something she let them do or asked them to do. *I should not have let them go do that. I should not have let them drive. I should not have bought a motorcycle for them.* As Mommas, we do our absolute best. Being a momma is a mixture of trying to simultaneously overprotect and also giving our children the space, they need to blossom. Before their death, we dealt with many of these decisions on a daily basis. If this is your case, I want you to listen: You are *not* at fault for your child's death. If you would have known the outcome, you would have protected your child—but you did not know. You did nothing wrong for allowing your child to live a life full of memories. You were being a *great* Momma.

What ifs are paramount with guilt as well. *What if I would have called? What if I would have gone by their house? What if I would have made him go to the doctor?* I actually had one what-if: *What if I would have been the person on night duty, the night Kaleb passed?* I believed as you, Mommas, that somehow, we could have changed the outcome. That by doing something more, our child would still be with us. As Mommas, we believe we can change the outcome of anything. That is the nurturing part of us. It is the protective instinct all of us as Mommas have.

A while back, I heard a momma talk about teenagers and young adults and to remember when we ourselves were teenagers. I am adding a little, but it went something like this: We wanted our parents to be less strict, we wanted the freedom to do what we wanted. We were taught right and wrong from our parents, but guess what we did? We did what we wanted because we believed we knew what was best for us. We believed our parents were the dumbest individuals in the world. If our parents asked us to do something, if we felt like it, we would do it; if we didn't feel like it, it was not going to happen. For mommas who suffer from guilt where you believe you could have done more, think of what I just stated. Tough love moment: There is nothing we could have done to change the outcome.

Some mommas say regarding their child loss, "I would feel guilty, to live life or be happy after losing them." Momma, I get it—I truly do. What the hell do you have to live for; how could you be happy and know that you buried your child. I know you don't want to hear this and it is cliché, but neither your child nor anyone in your life believe you should live a life of misery after your loss. Momma, I said this earlier: I have no clue why we were the chosen ones to lose a child. I don't know why we have to go through what we are going through, but I *damn* sure know we deserve to find some kind of happy. The idea of being happy may not be what it was at one time—hell, *we* are not who we once were—but you, Momma, deserve to live a wonderful life. You deserve to honor your child every day and smile when you think of them.

I know if you could have, you would have given your own life to save your child. This is us as Mommas—this is what pushes us every day when we feel like quitting. It is our drive and our primal instinct to protect our babies at any cost. But it's time to stop blaming yourself. It is time to pick yourself up and acknowledge that you, not doing something or having an instinct, has no direct link to why your child passed. It's time, Momma, to not live with the guilt anymore.

Now I know some of you Mommas are saying, "There is no way I will ever get over the guilt. It is my fault, and I can't live with it." I want you to think of this: How many times have people done things in your life that have hurt you? They have done things that made no sense, and you were in such shock and disbelief that someone could do something so horrible. We have forgiven these individuals, so why can't we forgive ourselves? If you find yourself not being able to get over the grief, even after I just talked about it, today I want you to forgive *yourself.* I want you to take the guilt in, own it, and tell yourself—today I will forgive myself and let it go.

The problem with holding on to the guilt is that you cannot move forward this way. Momma, you will stay stuck right where you are. If nothing I have mentioned is working and you have given it time to process, I want you to seek out and research a therapist who can actually help you with your guilt. I do not believe that therapy is perfect for everything dealing with child loss, but guilt will eat you alive. Guilt is one of the hardest stages to move on from, and the hardest to forgive yourself for. If you truly want to move forward and have a relationship with the new journey you are on, you have to move forward in all aspects of grief, including guilt.

Anger and Bargaining

Anger and bargaining... This is where I lived for a long time— *very* long time. Not only was I a joy to be around, but I was angry at everyone (This was meant to be humorous). This anger was directed toward mommas who I would see getting annoyed with their child, ignoring their child, posting toxic social media posts, talking about how annoyed they were with their child, or maybe wishing they didn't have a child. "Hello, you sorry (explicit work that starts with an "a") Mom who does not deserve a child—I *lost* my child and I would give *anything* to have them back." "You piece of (explicit word that begins with an "s")." Am I close to how you are feeling? *Oh,* I was so mad—I lost friends and would give dirty looks to anyone I believed was being a horrible mother.

What I found—and what you as a Momma need to remember—is that we all had those bad days. When our child was with us, we had those days where we would lose our mind about the daily tasks of being Momma. We never know what another person is going through. Being angry at these moms is all part of losing our child, and it's normal to be thinking this way. Our energy and thoughts need to be spent on something more... something that is all about *us* for a change.

There was one person who pissed me off to my limits. I cursed them and turned my back on them in a moment's time. The thought of them would make my skin crawl and my blood boil. That person was God. Holy crap, how do I say that?! But that was my truth, and I was pissed at God for a long time. I could not wrap my head around why... Why did you choose *me* to have to deal with this? Why did you let me experience the trauma of my Kaleb's birth, give both of us two years to live together, then take it all away?! How dare you take him after our two years together and leave me here to suffer! Why did you choose *me* to suffer? No, I was not the missionary in school, but I was a *good* person—I took care of Kaleb and loved him unconditionally. I didn't abuse drugs or alcohol, I went to work, I served my community—why God... Why?!

It took many years, and it has not been too far back now that I decided to make peace. I had to stop asking why and start repairing myself and my faith. I have my reasons as to how and why I started to repair my faith—but the biggest reason was that I could not imagine a life where my ending did not have me reunited with my Kaleb. Although I have a lot more life to live, it is good to know that when it is my time, I will have him waiting for me.

Momma, your anger is a direct correlation to your child loss. You want others to feel as much pain as you are feeling. That's why the anger comes. There are many things that you can be angry about—I gave you two, but there are thousands. Next time you get angry, I want you to pause and think about *why* you are angry. Where is your anger coming from and is your anger from your grief? Once the anger comes out, you can't take it back. Your words and your anger can cause more damage to friendships and family members than you will know, especially right now. When you are feeling anger, take a deep breath and find your quiet place—think about where all the anger is coming from, and why it is directed toward that specific person. By analyzing it, you can learn the deeper meaning of your anger which, in turn, helps you move forward.

Depression

Many of you suffer from depression, which is also a stage, Mommas. This is normal, you just lost your beloved child. I don't know a momma who has lost a child and has *not* gone through depression, unless they did not know they were going through it at the time. That is why depression is one of the stages of grief.

I went through it just like you, Mommas. I refused to eat at first, I just did not feel like eating and was not hungry at all. It was a choice not to eat, but it wasn't because I wanted nothing more than to lay in bed. I did not want anyone or anything to bother me but my faithful sidekick, Katie (my miniature dachshund). I had lots of family and friends wanting to show their support and be there for me, but it did not matter. I did not want to get out of bed. I did nothing but cry and I can remember crying so much I could not cry anymore. I'm sure you know Momma by now that not being able to cry anymore is truly a thing. I did not care about how I looked or when the last time I took a shower was. I just wanted to curl up and be by myself because I did not believe anyone understood what I was going through. I just wanted my Kaleb back, and that could not happen.

I was so exhausted from all of the emotions I dealt with each day that I would fall right to sleep. My mind is a busy one—it is going full-out every minute of every day when I am awake. So, I would try and process everything when I was awake. When I would lie down, I would fall right to sleep. My entire body was tired. I would sleep so much, but when I would wake, I would still be exhausted. Some of you Mommas are experiencing the opposite—you cannot sleep because your minds are in overdrive constantly thinking about everything. This happens to many mommas as well. Because of this, you are more irritable, and everything is multiplied one hundred percent. Your emotions are so strong, and you don't believe you will make it through. Well you will,

Momma—and as hard as it is now to believe, you will indeed come out of the black hole currently enveloping you.

Depression is a real thing, and it is *definitely* a real thing with child loss. Many mommas are going through depression long after their child has passed. I won't put a time limit on how long you are going to be depressed, because everyone is different. Many individuals talk about being depressed for six months to a year after their child is gone. I could not tell you the exact day I woke up and was not depressed, but eventually it happened. I think it was gradual, and it took a lot of time and willpower to come back from the dark hole I was spiraling down into. Although this is normal, I want you to seek a therapist, and fast if you have any thoughts of suicide.

Real talk Mommas: I can remember thinking I had nothing to live for. I can remember processing in my brain that if something happened to me, it would be alright because I could see Kaleb again. I never thought about killing myself, but I was in an extremely dark place. I know now that I probably should have found the right therapist to help me, but I was worried about the stigma about getting help and truly believed no one could help me or would understand. Learning moment Mommas: Don't be me. Yes, I have come through child loss, and on the outside at the time I appeared to have my shit together—but why go through that struggle if you can seek help and get through it faster? Your family and friends have already lost one precious soul—they can't lose you too!

Loneliness and Reflection

We get to a point in our child loss where we start to reflect on everything in our life. We usually do it alone, which in turn makes us feel like we truly *are* alone. It is part of the stages of grief, Momma—loneliness and reflection. I still to this day do not understand how we want to be left alone, but then when we are we feel *so* alone. Being lonely is not always someone not being around, it can also have a deeper meaning. I did not feel anyone understood what was going on or how I was feeling. I felt like I was alone, in my own little world where I was alienated from everyone since no one could understand me. Although a lot of people did not understand what I was going through, in my mind, I made this loneliness worse. I did not seek out anyone who had lost a child before me, and I did not try to find someone who would understand. I just sat in my house, with my little dog, and reflected.

Reflection, of course, is about our child—but for me, it was also about reflecting on my life. My life... What a train wreck. Not only did I lose my child, but I also divorced Brian because he did not understand what I was going through. While I was reflecting, I realized just *how much* I played the victim in everything in my life—including my child loss. I had somehow made my child loss all about me and my feelings. I thought nothing about the feelings of others or how they were hurting. Tough love moment: Momma, stop playing the victim. Learn from my mistakes and realize you are not a victim. Putting yourself in the victim mindset allows you to be victimized repeatedly. By doing this, it makes any memory of your child negative. It takes away everything leading up to the day they passed. We must hold on to those *good* memories, because they are what will keep us going on the bad days. We must honor our child to keep moving forward.

As I sat and reflected, I realized the life I was living was not the life I wanted to be remembered for. I was in no way shape or form a bad person. I served my community, respected my elders, and was loyal to my family and friends—but I knew I could respect myself more, and do and *be* more in life. When you are alone and you contemplate your life, you may not like what you see. If you are hard on yourself (like I am), this makes it even more difficult. You cannot change the way you lived your life before your child loss, but you *can* change the way you live your life after your child loss. Do not live in the past, instead look forward to your future and where your life needs to be.

I decided when I was reflecting that I was not going to let the loss of my Kaleb define who I was in life. I was not going to allow myself to forget, or have others forget, Kaleb. That is another worry we have— that we will always remember our child. But as time goes on, those around us will forget them. I was determined not to let that happen, so I started to brainstorm my life and try things I wasn't even sure I'd like. I became obsessed with the way my life should be—probably more than I should have, but it was my new goal. I worked and decided what

I would do to have those around me remember my child. I started to seek out mommas who recently had lost their child, helping them. From experience, I did some things I didn't like. Once, I went to a party for a friend's child. I, of course, did not have another child—but I went anyway, to get out and do more. Man, that was rough. I felt like a dirty old lady who preyed on young kids. Not the story at all, but that was how I felt—and that was also the first (and last) time I attended a child's party. The experience made me uncomfortable, so I chose not to do it again.

Experience new things—you never know, you may enjoy them. Our life will never be the same. We have changed from the very beginning when our child died and go through a roller coaster of emotions from that day onward. One thing we can control is what we choose to do and how we choose to live our life. Stop doing things you hate doing and try new things you think you might enjoy. You will also learn that things you used to enjoy may not provide you with enjoyment anymore. Reconstruct your life to what you enjoy now versus what you enjoyed in the past.

Acceptance

They say acceptance is the last stage of grief. Wow, right? Accept that Kaleb is gone? That's kind of hard to do. I have accepted that he is not *with* me, but I don't know if I will ever fully accept his death. I have accepted that I will always remember his death like it was yesterday. I have accepted that my life has forever been changed. I have accepted that I am the one who has to make the choice to keep moving forward. I have accepted that I am the person who will keep my child's memory alive. I don't really know what acceptance means, to tell you the truth. To accept the death of my son and move on? No, we don't move on, we move forward—and that, Mommas, is exactly how it should be.

Remember, there is no end to our child's life really—our child will always be a part of us for the rest of our life. We all go through these stages of grief—sometimes directly as I have listed, and sometimes we skip or don't go through them at all. The decision to put one foot in front of the other is one we make every day. The truth is, we can slip back into any of these stages at any time. It does not matter whether it has been a year or 20 years. At 11 years, if I allow myself, I could slip back into any stage of grief. Because Momma, there is no day that you are going to be free from grief. There is no secret formula that is going to make you stop feeling the pain. It is on *you* to decide how you will move forward after your loss.

If you find yourself moving through the stages of grief and become stuck, evaluate why you can't move forward. What is holding you back? What is keeping you from stepping forward? What do you need to *help* you move forward?

If you find yourself slipping back into a stage, what happened? Are you doing something different? Did another traumatic event happen in your life? Figure out what happened and give yourself the time and space you need to rise from where you are. This is going to happen, and guess what? It is completely normal.

I know this chapter may have been blah, but I believe to understand and move forward in grief, we must know where we are starting from. Give yourself permission to go through each stage. Give yourself permission to go back to a stage in life, because it may happen. Note where you believe you are starting from and let's move forward.

The most difficult thing is the decision to act. The rest is merely tenacity.

–Amelia Earhart

Chapter 5:

Can I Be Fixed?

After reading the last chapter, you are probably wondering, *Can I be fixed?*! That truly is hard to answer. If you feel being fixed entails going back to the way your life once was, then no—you can't be fixed. Your life will never be the way it was before your child left. It's about more than losing your child—the way you view the world, your morals, and what you value most will ultimately change. This is true with trauma in general—mommas find themselves not fitting in where they once did.

Remember those awkward teen years? We did a lot of crazy stuff and tried new things, bad and good. We tried different clothing; we tried different sports or liked what our friends liked. Those experiences and years molded us into the adults we became. Our personalities, our likes, and our dislikes were all formed from these years. In our earlier years, they were of course formed by our parents. Once we have lost a child, our body is in shock mode. We begin questioning not only us as parents, but our life in general. We realize just how short life truly is and how precious the short time we are here really is. As a Momma to an angel, we realize just how truly dumb the small things that gripped us or ticked us off were, and how they really don't matter. We start to fear just how much we don't recognize ourselves anymore. We start to fear the future.

When I started to think about my life before Kaleb's death, I was ashamed of who I was. I was the, "It's all about me" person. I thought

I could do no wrong and the only person who deserved to come before me was Kaleb. I was on marriage number 3—yes, at 31—and divorcing number 3. It wasn't until I was all alone with the loss of my Kaleb that I could really see what was in front of me. I was alone, in a big house, without my child. It gets pretty quiet and lonely when you have just an amazing little dog named Katie to take care of (and I would eventually add Ali, my other pup, in a few months).

I can tell you that every demon I ever had came out. So not only was I having to deal with my child loss, but I also was having to deal with demons from my past. It was a complete shit show. I became more depressed, and I only associated with my parents or with coworkers when I was at work. I was ashamed of who I had been and how little I cared about anyone's feelings—or life in general. The loss of Kaleb had turned on a toxicity inside me. Something to wake me up and tell me, *Hey guess what, you really suck.* It finally clicked that there was more to life than how I was living. I was going to be more; I was going to make Kaleb proud of me. I just did not know where to begin and was scared of change.

Momma, you may find yourself in the same place I was in. You are going down a black hole, and each day you seem to be slipping further and further into it. You are going to review your life, trust me—it just happens because you are in that low and dark place. If you feel that you suck like I did, remember that right now it is going to seem 10 times worse than it truly is. That is part of your grief process with losing your child. But you *do* have a choice to change it. Moving forward and changing the person you once were seems scary, but it can be done—and it *has* to be done or you will remain in the same spot you are now.

I got to a point where I knew I could not live another 50 years feeling the way I did. In general, if you live to be 80, how many years do you have? Can you live where you are at right now for that many years? I'll answer that for you Momma—heck no, you can't. Tell yourself today is the day you are going to move forward and not fear the future. Today, you will start planning for your future and create the life you want to live. Nobody can make the decision for you: you must want it, you must know it, and you have to live it. You are an amazing woman and truly special. As I said before, I have no idea why we must go through child loss; it truly is a mystery... but here we are.

The truth is, though, we are not broken and there is nothing to fix. You had a life-changing event, and our bodies react exactly the way they are meant to react. We just must figure out how to live again. I know I make it sound so easy, but it's not—and it's a long road. Your determination and willpower will guide you on those days you just can't go anymore. But I am going to give you some paths to try. These paths worked for me, and I know they will also work for you. The only catch is, you can't try one day and choose not to the next. You must put in the work, and it's not hard work. Somedays, it may seem like work; but I can promise those hard days will happen less as time goes on. Make up your mind and let's do it.

I am a firm believer that we must write it, read it, think it, hear it, speak it, and live it. In order to fully find a relationship with life and to move forward, we must have these elements. Taking one out disrupts moving forward. We must have them all, and here is how I suggest you start.

Moving Forward with Your Life

Journaling

We all must know where we are starting from. I want you to go online or to a bookstore and find a journal that jumps out at you—one that makes you feel something. Mine is a leather journal with braided sides and etching on it. I personally like having something in my hands, putting pen to paper the old-fashioned way. You may find it easier to keep a folder on your computer. How you choose to journal doesn't matter, as long as you are journaling.

Your first entry is your story. I want you to spend time on this entry; maybe it will take you a couple of days but write down everything. Tell the story of your child's death. Write down all of your emotions—the rage, the sadness, and even some of the emotions you are feeling that you are not proud of. This is your true starting point, so make it count. Believe in your heart this is the last time you will be in this spot emotionally and mentally.

Now that you have released your story and have it documented, I want you to keep your journal close to you. Each time you have thoughts of your child, write about them. Write about the good or the bad times that come to mind. The idea is to write it down, thereby releasing it from your mind.

I personally also like writing down quotes. If a quote speaks to me, I will write it in my journal. Many of my journal entries are quotes. You can choose to do this or not, it depends on what you want your journal to contain. Personally, I like to include a mixture of negative and positive thoughts adorned with positive quotes. I like going back and looking at those quotes sometimes as well to remember them.

I want to describe how you advance your journaling now. When you are having a bad day, I want you to write it down. Write down what caused you to feel this emotion, and you can ask yourself these questions:

- What were you thinking about?

- Where were you at?

- Who were you talking to?

- How was your day before the emotion started?

Get all of this written down. Then next, you will look for the trigger (what caused it?). Was it a smell, was it the place you were at, or was it the conversation you were having? Dig deep and evaluate where the emotion came from. Yes, it came from you; yes, you were talking about your child; but emotion is usually triggered by a specific incident or a specific thing. By evaluating each time, you feel the emotion, you can avoid those incidents that are making you feel the way you feel. You will be able to change your mindset around the incident by changing the way you view it. If you can't avoid it, you will at least understand the trigger.

Evaluating Our Thoughts

Part of grieving is thinking about the process itself. We must think about our loss and where we are at physically, mentally, and emotionally. When we have a traumatic event, our mind will try to protect us from the negative experience. We either disassociate ourselves from the event and push it away or we ruminate generally on only the negative aspects of our child's life. From speaking with mommas, I know they put a bandage on their grief. If we don't think about it, or hide it away, we don't have to feel it. What I find from doing this is we mask it to a point where it becomes triggered by an event, by speaking about it, or even by looking at a picture. We have a flood of emotions and are inconsolable because everything is coming out all at once. After our breaking point, we put the bandage back on the grief again and wait for the next time the wound opens up. I know you can see how unhealthy this is.

The second thing mommas do is they think about their loss all the time and become cynical, angry, sad, or maybe even associate their child in general as negative. I've seen that mommas who do this are extremely depressed or—as I say—angry with the world. They take on a victim role. Life did this to them, and now their life is horrible. Their whole life centers around the loss of their child. Their life story becomes their child's death, and no more. This is unhealthy too, but I am sure you can see it.

Tough love moment: If you are set on either one of those ways to deal with your loss, put this book down, for it is not the book for you. If you recognize yourself in one of the above but know that is not what you want—that your life is more than your child loss—the good news is that you can change the way you think. It is so easy for our mindset to generally become negative after the loss of a child, and I will not pretend to think my mindset wasn't completely negative. It is not whether our mindset turns south: it's what we do to rise above the negativity.

Replacing Negative Thoughts with Positive Thoughts

We talked above about evaluating our thoughts in certain situations, but there are other things you can do when you find your mind is in a negative place. One way of working through a negative thought is by immediately replacing it with a positive thought. When I would first wake up in the morning and automatically go to my negative place. My Kaleb was gone, and my life was miserable. *You know* how we can think when we first wake up. I had to literally think of something positive. As new as my loss was, I had already trained my brain to think my Kaleb was negative and my life was negative because he was no longer physically with me.

This is why journaling is important in your child loss. It allows you to write every thought down and ponder them. These two practices are so important in the process.

Creating an Affirmation

I mentioned that in the morning I would start my day by a negative thought and replace it with a positive thought. Have I told you guys yet that I am not a morning person? The thought of thinking more than I had to would be a chore. For all 365 days in a year, I do not want to think of something positive. So, I created an affirmation. You may be just like me, not able to think of all this positive stuff at first. It took me a while, but what I would do was create an affirmation that fit my situation and my personality. An affirmation is declaring something to yourself or possibly the world. It is usually something positive that you're going to do or think—something positive that you believe deep down about yourself or your life, and maybe both. I took the time to create an affirmation—not a few words, but a sentence that I understood. Each morning when I would get out of bed I would say, "I have already lived my worst day. Each day after will be better than that day." It made sense to me, it was true to me, and it worked for what I wanted to do. I didn't believe *everything* was going to be okay at first, but I knew my day would not be as bad as the day that Kaleb died. When I woke up, I would say my affirmation—usually more than once. If I started to get a negative thought in my head, I would simply close my eyes and say my affirmation. Eventually, I believed my affirmation completely.

Take out a piece of paper or open up your computer and write an affirmation that is true to you... something you believe or want to believe but are having a hard time believing at the moment. Write it down and try to write more than a few words but enough where you can remember it. If you don't have the time to write down an affirmation right now, use mine or find one online that rings true to you. Read it out loud in the mornings and read it out loud when you have a negative thought. I know it may seem strange, and you may be thinking, *This is not going to work for me*. I can tell you from my own experience—they *do* work, and they *will* help you.

Talking About Your Child with Others

Every time you need to say it out loud, really hear what you are saying—this is another way to help you in your child loss. When I lost Kaleb, I could barely talk about losing him. It was so hard to even think about it, much less actually *talk* about him and how I was feeling since his passing. So, I did what anyone would do... I stopped talking about the thing that was upsetting me. Hell, I wasn't raised to be dumb. So of course, wrong answer again. One of the worst things us Mommas can do is think it is better to stop talking about our child. It is quite literally toxic to not talk about what is on our mind. I did eventually start talking to mommas online about my Kaleb again. I could text about Kaleb, and everything would be fine. I thought I was doing great! I was going through the process, and it was getting easier. I had told my story so many times to other mommas and was helping them in the process. Life was getting better, and I felt like I had a purpose or a place where I was needed.

I went to instructor school. (Yeah, I've done many things). For your general instructor certification, I had to write a lesson plan on a specific subject that deals with law enforcement. Since I was impacted by Peer Support when I lost my Kaleb, that was my subject. I learned so much about it, how to start a group, and what classes needed to be taken. I was going to start my instruction by having the class close their eyes, then I would tell them my nightmare and have them think about it, in the sense that it was their own family. During the class, we had to stand at the front of the classroom several times and speak about our project, teaching portions of it. So naturally, on my first try I was so nervous—I walked up to the front, managed to muster telling the class to close their eyes, and started telling my story. I choked up and started crying, and I had to pause to continue, then finally finish my story. When I had them open their eyes, they were speechless; the instructors teaching the class didn't know what to say. I apologized and they made me feel better by telling me that it had more of an impact, and it was powerful.

I was so pissed off with myself. Why in the hell did I break down when telling my story?! I had told it hundreds of times, to many different mommas. Why did this happen... dang, what was wrong with me?! Well quite frankly, nothing was wrong with me at all. Yes, I did tell my story many times, but I did not *speak* it in front of a class. Remember earlier, when I told you I stopped talking about Kaleb out loud because it upset me? I worked through writing about it, reading it, and thinking about it—but I refused to speak it. Mommas, part of moving forward is also talking about your child. You are keeping yourself from rebuilding your life if you hold this all in, and you are the person who is choosing to hide your child from the world. That is not fair to you or your child. I will talk about this more in another chapter—but if someone has a problem with it, tough shit. Your child is still as much a part of your life now than before they died. And to tell you the truth, your child's death has probably molded you into the person you are now, just like it did for me. If you are wondering, by the end of the instructor training, I had mastered talking about my experience with child loss and became a certified instructor.

Speaking about your child is important when moving forward. The event leading up to your child's death, maybe not so much—but your child. Talk about your child, Mommas. Some mommas feel that because their child is gone, that is it. We should not talk about our child, and we should not talk out loud to our child... and this is so far from the truth. Your child will always be part of you. They are a piece of your life, even if they are not physically here with you. Part of processing and moving forward is not forgetting. One of our biggest fears is people forgetting our child or forgetting all the memories ourselves. What better way to keep our memories alive and honor our child than talking about them?

Talk about funny times, great vacations, sports trips, graduations, driving lessons... There are so many beautiful memories. Pick all those memories because, even though they are not with us anymore, our child will appear closer to us. We do this with parents and grandparents after they have passed—so why is it so hard to do with our child? There is an easy answer to this: because it is out of order. Our child's death is not what was supposed to happen. Our child was supposed to bury *us*, as many people say, and you have probably heard that at least twice since your child's death. Yeah, our life kind of screwed up that whole life cycle thing but it is our truth. It is okay to talk about your child. Do not be ashamed or embarrassed about your child's death, feel guilty, or feel you need to just get over it. There is no getting over child loss, and I hope by this point in this book you understand that you aren't going to get over your child's death—but you *can* move forward and build a life you love.

Living Your Life Honoring Your Child and Yourself

Live it—this is my last step in the process. You have to live each day, honoring your child and working on truly knowing yourself. I think a big part of living the life I live now is from knowing myself. I discovered a lot in the process of losing my child. One thing I learned, which is hilarious to me, is that I'm an introvert. Did not know it until I was about 36 years old—but yep, I am. I wasn't shy growing up, I wasn't lazy when I didn't want to go out, and I wasn't mean to people, well maybe some. I just didn't want to be in a crowded room, with a bunch of people putting my senses into overdrive. And I was useless days after these gatherings because I was completely drained. Having learned this, I am better prepared for situations now; I know when I have had enough, and I know my limits. I learned I take on too many tasks at a time, trying to do all things for all people, then have just that *little bit* of time to do something for me. I am still working on this, but at least I can recognize when I am burning myself out and will stop and think about what I can change or what I need to give up. Now, whether I give it up or not is another story. I am a work in progress.

Those are just two of the things I learned about myself during this process. I know some of you are probably like, *How in the hell did you not know you were an introvert?* Yeah, it's a shocker for most people. As Mommas, we do and *are* everything for everyone. We mask our likes and dislikes and become what we are needed to become. When we become moms, our world stops, and our child's world becomes "our world," where we give more to the other half—our child. Understand that for most, traumatic events change morals, values, and beliefs. When other mommas say they will never be the same (or they never were the same), there is a lot of truth to that. When you believe you don't feel the same and you aren't the same person, you simply *aren't*. Don't think of it as a negative thing. I know it's not what you want to hear, and you were just fine living your life. We can't change it, though, so embrace the change—this does not mean you have to like it. Be open to your mindset changing and be open to rebuilding your life after the loss of your child. Some days, that's all you can give and other days, you can take on major steps in the process. Just don't give up, Momma, and keep pushing.

I asked in the beginning of this chapter if you can be fixed. No, I don't believe you can be fixed, because there is nothing *wrong* with you. I urge you to take a personality test, even if you have taken one before. See where you are now, compared to where you were. This may give you an understanding of how much you have changed or why you feel the life you are living doesn't fulfill you. Be careful in the beginning stages of your grief, though. Sometimes your grief will reveal your answers, and sometimes we will guess using what we believed the answer would be before our child loss. The best time to take this test would be when you are in a good place, and know you are ready for change. This gives you a clear mindset to be completely honest with the answers and yourself.

If you have never taken a personality test, it gives you a great starting point. It gives you an understanding of who you are and why you believe what you believe. If for some reason you take the personality test and months down the road, you believe that it does not match who you are, take it again to see if possibly your grief was overshadowing the real you. It could be that your morals, values, and beliefs have changed the further you are into your loss. I waited over five years before I took one. Although this is probably not ideal, at this stage I was most accepting of who I was.

Who you were and what you believed in totally changed after the loss of your child. You are lost and feel alone because your old life is not aligned with the new one you have been forced to endure. It's like throwing a softball player into a gymnastic meet, putting a teacher in the role of a baker, or a first-time mom in the role of a momma. We eventually will figure it out, but shit's not going to be easy at first. It will take you time, practice, and a true understanding of the craft. Yes, being a Momma is a craft. It's one of the hardest jobs there is.

With your trauma comes changes to many aspects of your life. The way I viewed many things had changed. This is just part of the process, and I am okay with that. I like the saying, "I cut the fat," meaning I cut off all things that I did not need and were not perfect for the life I wanted to live after my child loss. One of the most important things I learned was that life is way too short to live with negativity surrounding me. So, I cut that fat—and I cut a lot of it. This included family and friends who did nothing but bring negativity to my life. This leads me to the next chapter: Family, Friends, and Children.

The healing power of even the most microscopic exchange with someone who knows in a flash precisely what you're talking about because she experienced that thing too cannot be overestimated.

–Cheryl Strayed

Chapter 6:

Family, Friends, and Children

Friends

Have you ever thought about the cycle of life? From the time we are born, we have this learned notion that this is the way our life progresses: we are born, we're toddlers, then we're tweens and teens, we go through young adulthood, reach middle age, then old age, and at the end we die. We may be taught this, or we may make the educated decision that this is what happens during our time on Earth. But what if one of those pieces are taken out? Instead of going through young adulthood, you pass away from cancer, or from a car wreck, or God forbid a toddler dies of cancer or dies as a baby at birth. People lose their mind; they don't know how to act or what to say. It's not what is supposed to happen?! Our children are supposed to bury *us*. I can remember my cousin sitting down with me at Kaleb's viewing and asking me how I was. All I could think to say was, "This just sucks." I don't think I've ever spoken truer words.

I can say, there were so many people—family and friends—who came to support me in the weeks following Kaleb's death. So many, in fact, that I can't remember—and only remember when I take out his funeral book and look at the names. Hell, there are some names I don't even recognize. I'm sure those were people Kaleb had touched in passing or one of his friend's parents from his special needs daycare. I truly appreciate all of them for their support and am grateful for each and every one of them. So, if you are reading this book because you knew Kaleb—thank you from the bottom of my heart.

I had so many friends before Kaleb passed, though many of them were put on hold once Kaleb was born because of his 24/7 care needs. I still considered them friends, and they understood. It's what happens with *all* friends as marriages, babies, and life starts to take over. Instead of a group of friends, we become family pods. Sometimes our family pods drift apart, though, leaving only memories of the times we once had. I can say I experienced this twice in my life—once when Kaleb was born, and when Kaleb died.

I don't think any of my friends woke up the day Kaleb died and said they were never going to talk to me again. As shitty as the world is right now, people aren't that shitty. But I did not understand what was happening to my friends, and the friends I thought would always be there for me were nowhere to be found.

It's been over 11 years now—some friends I still don't talk to, and years after Kaleb's death some have walked back into my life. I know some of you are probably thinking, *How could you possibly let them back into your life, when they weren't there for you when you needed them the most?* Through forgiveness and understanding, I have let some of them back in.

I am not going to tell you what to do—you have been told that enough—but I want you to remember the cycle of life. This cycle is ingrained in our head our whole life, and we would think nothing of it if our cycle wasn't destroyed. We had to bury our own *child*. At the same time, we are in shock, our friends are also in shock. Worldwide, millions of children die, but it is still a small percentage when you rank it next to the billions of people who live in the world. Although now I know several women who have lost a child, I was blind to it until it happened to me. The likelihood that your friends have experienced child loss themselves or know someone who has lost a child is slim. They are just as shocked as you are and must process the grief as well.

The meaning of "fight or flight" became an understanding that I now know all too well. Fight or flight, in simple terms, is a person's bodily reaction to an event. In this case, it would be the death of our child. You will have friends who will disappear, and you will have friends who will be by your side. It will surprise you who stays, and it will surprise you who goes.

At the time of my loss, I was working at a Drug Task Force. We worked with several different counties around South Georgia. We all thought that life didn't get any better, and were all so "bullheaded," as I called it. We were close enough to work together and have Christmas parties, but not close enough to barbecue every weekend with our families.

On the way to the hospital the night Kaleb died, I opened my phone to call my old boss, Jamy, because we had a new boss, Bahan, who had just started. I wanted to tell him a little of what was happening just so he knew I would not be at work. Instead, I called another officer, Will, someone I worked with at the Nashville Police Department. I apologized for calling him so early, and that I was really trying to call Jamy. Will asked me what was wrong, and I told him what was going on. I hung up with him and immediately called Jamy. Things progressed, as I spoke about previously. And as we were walking out the front doors to the waiting room to go home, there was a familiar face as Will stood up. Once I got off the phone with him, he had come to the hospital and waited until we left. Will and I would ride together when I worked in Nashville, Georgia, but I would never consider us close. Will was a fighter—he took whatever beliefs he had and tucked them away to just be there for me. I never would have expected him to be there for me, but I gained so much respect for him after this act of kindness.

In the days to come when I was not working, my coworkers would be pallbearers for my son and would also come to my house every night after work, just to sit and be with me. Most of the time we sat and laughed together, talking about everything you could possibly think of—but they were just there for *me*. They did not know what to say or how to act, so they did the best thing they could possibly do—be themselves. It was what I needed after an exhausting day of being a grieving Momma.

My new boss, Bahan—he came too. He would become someone I looked up to, and I mimicked his management style years later. Bahan would call me into his office, we'd shut the door, and he would just ask me how I was doing. I am sure there were ulterior motives to make sure my head was on straight, and I would not get anyone hurt, but regardless, he sat and listened to anything I wanted to say. I often look back at everything that was thrown on him so soon and wonder how in the heck did he do it? It wouldn't be until years later, that I would experience the loss of an agent as a new supervisor. Maneuvering through tragedy and keeping my unit together during such a time was absolutely horrible. To this day, on every anniversary of Kaleb's death, he will text me and let me know he is thinking about me. It's nothing special, no words of wisdom, just that he is thinking about me; but it lets me know that he remembers, and Kaleb is not forgotten.

Not six months later, one of the individuals I worked with named Jason had a child who was diagnosed with Leukemia. The Drug Task Force didn't receive the funding needed to keep it open, so it was closing. Man, when it rains it pours, but I will say—Addie beat cancer and we all made it through the closing of the task force. "Biz," as I call him, would continue working with me a few years later while everyone else would scatter to work in different areas. We all formed a bond from those last months at the task force, and though we've since gone our separate ways, our shared bond will always be remembered.

I had a few friends who I remember being there for me. Again, I don't think I will ever remember them all, but I remember Jen. She had a son a little bit older than Kaleb at the time. I can remember her calling and saying through her tears, "Girl, what the hell." All I could say was, "I don't know." Jen was there for Kaleb's traumatic birth and now she was experiencing his death. Not only was she grieving this little child, but I can also imagine she was thinking about her own son who was only a year older than Kaleb. Jen had her own family and was trying to be the best momma she could be, but she was there because she wanted to bear the storm with me.

I had many friends who were there for me, and there were some I just *knew* would be around—but they were not. I had two old beat partners who I just knew would be there for me. I just knew I would see those familiar faces at any moment... but they were not seen. Some of them I see in passing, and I don't hold grudges or think any less of them. For a long time, I was angry. I was angry at the people I shared so much time with and cared about. I was crushed, and I questioned the friendships I had. As time went on though, I just let it go. Though I didn't understand it, I was worrying about stuff that I could not change, and it did not matter. In the big picture of life in general, what does it matter?

Years later, I actually worked with one of the individuals who I just knew would be there for me but was not. I never mentioned this to him, though, and never treated him any different. He brought it up one day and apologized for not being there for me. He said he could not imagine losing a child and did not know what to say or do for me. He had children—they were older, but he had children. In his mind, he could not bring himself to even think about what I was going through, so he took the flight mode—or in other words, he was MIA. You would never know it if you saw us together now. We don't talk about that time; he listens when I talk about my son, but we talked about Kaleb's passing just once.

When it comes to your friends, you are going to find that the people you would least expect are the ones who will surprise you the most. They choose to stay by your side, even when they don't know what to do. They just know they simply want to *be* there for you. When I say you will have people who will stand by your side and not know what to say to you, I mean it literally.

Case in point, I can remember meeting with the coroner about some of the paperwork I needed to get. I knew him well because I was in law enforcement. We talked for a few minutes, and he was deeply moved, almost to tears. He knew all of Kaleb's issues—I mean, he had Kaleb's *medical* record. As he talked, I could see the tears forming in his eyes. I was being stoic and would remain that way, for he wasn't in my circle. And then out of nowhere he said, "You couldn't have done that for the rest of your life." WHAT?! Did this man really just *say* that? The anger was boiling up, and I said, "Yes, I *could* have." I guess my anger wasn't strong enough because he came back with, "No, you couldn't have." What the hell! Was I really hearing this right?! Of course, I could have! He was my damn son, my *life*. Holy, explicit word with an "f," was I in an alternate universe where it's okay for my child to die because he had a lot of special needs? I was speechless. This was the first time I heard the crazy stuff people say when they try to figure out *what* to say when you lose your child.

I would later hear the norm: "You're young, you can have more kids," or "How are you doing?" To this second question, my response in my head was, "Pretty damn shitty." But instead, "Doing good," or "I'm okay" would always come out of my mouth. Later, I would question whether I am the one to blame for the stupid questions. I mean, if I told them I was crappy, would they have asked me again? Probably not, because there is no follow-up to that.

I've learned from years of questions that friends just want you to be happy again. They want you to go back to the way you once were. They don't understand that you will never *be* that chic again, though. We must realize that the only way to get help from our friends is to tell them what we need. Have that deep conversation with them, as hard as it may be. It's going to go one of two ways: they will stand by you, or they will disappear—just like the first initial friends did when you lost your child. But that is okay because as I have mentioned, after trauma the people who mean the most to you may not fit into your new journey. We must find our new circle. Some of our circle may stay the same, but we will bring in a whole new tribe as well. I am bonded to the mothers who I have met in the last 11-plus years and would have never bonded with them before my loss. Not that they were bad people, but our lives would have never crossed paths. I have also experienced this with individuals who have no idea what it is like to lose a child, but they just want to be there for me throughout the years as I grieve. Momma, if you feel alone, open up and let those people in. They have truly been a gift given to me, like I know they will be a gift for you. People are placed in our life at the perfect time—it's not a coincidence they are there, because their purpose is to help you through your next chapter.

As for the people that are MIA, the missing friends—let them go. We have enough trauma drama in our life right now, so why add more anger and stress into our lives? Christina Aguilera said it best (Auguilera 1999), "They say if you love something, let it go, If it comes back it's yours. That's how you know. It's for keeps, yeah, it's for sure. And you're ready and willin' to give me more than." Let it go, Momma.

Maybe they will come back later with a big explanation, and maybe they won't. Either way is okay. And I urge you to be cautious when they *do* come back. Don't let them come back in your good times easily, if in your bad times they couldn't hang. Keep that in mind when you decide who will be a part of your new journey.

Family

Family, I have learned, can be your greatest or worst supporter. There are just so many factors at play, and it really depends on if you have a close family or not. The only problem is that when they don't help with the rebuilding of your life, you can't get rid of them as easily. But either way, you can distance yourself from the negative.

I think the first—and most important—person to mention is my ex-husband. For some of you this may be your husband, significant other, or your child's father. "Complicated" is the word that comes to mind right away. Not only are *you* grieving, but your other half is too. To make matters worse, the two of you are probably grieving differently.

Brian was an awesome dad to Kaleb. I could count on him any time to help out, to take him to appointments, and to love Kaleb with all his heart. He was big into videos and pictures, which looking back on now, I am so glad he was. Since Kaleb had cerebral palsy, Brian was a researcher—looking up all the newest and greatest electronics and techniques to help with this disability. I had extremely high expectations for him, as my own dad was extremely hands-on with my brothers, sister, and me.

Our problems started when Kaleb was born. After the traumatic birth and his diagnosis, I became the one who believed Kaleb could do anything and he was going to surprise everyone; Brian became the one who was accepting of what he couldn't do, and I felt he did not want to push Kaleb enough. We started to drift apart at a certain point, and I filed for divorce. Though everything was settled, we still decided to try again and fix what had been broken since the night Kaleb died. After the loss of Kaleb, we stayed together for a little while longer—I truly can't remember how long. We even tried to get pregnant after Kaleb, but it never happened for us. Personally, I just wanted to be alone to think and he was more willing to sit and talk with others. Instead of grieving together, we began to grieve apart. This happened until eventually he retired from the military and moved back to Wisconsin to begin his schooling to be an occupational therapist, which he still does today. On Kaleb's death day, most years we will talk—nothing extremely chatty, but we catch up on life and our thoughts about Kaleb. We both have moved on with significant others but have formed a friendship through the experience we shared together.

Marriage and Divorce

This is not a how-to-not-get-divorced book, but I *do* want to talk about it. I have read so many crazy statistics stating that up to 50% of people get divorced and 16% who lose a child will divorce (Lach's Legacy 2022). Though I've seen even higher, I will leave it at that. Although I know several parents who have divorced, I also know several who have not.

Laura and Fred have been married for years—I knew Fred from working with him during my Task Force days. I think their marriage is the definition of a perfect marriage. Although Fred says it wasn't always perfect because of things he did (very rare admission ladies), they worked on their marriage daily. They have the sweetest child, and all have huge hearts. They lost their son, Jonathan, to suicide after Kaleb had passed.

I remember reaching out to Fred to tell him how sorry I was, and to tell him it never really goes away, but to lean on his family. He made a little small chat, but nothing major. This was back in 2017, and I can say that family is the closest family I have ever met. They leaned on each other, they still celebrated, and they still live their lives with meaning. None of it was easy and each of them have their bad days, but they choose to live and use their voice. They founded Jon's Mission for 22, Inc., a group that supports other veteran's families who lost a child due to suicide. They educate and raise money every year for these families, and travel all over to tell the story of these veterans. Are they healed? There is no healing from child loss, but they choose every day not to take anything for granted and they celebrate Jon's life, not his death.

To say that everyone is going to get a divorce because they are grieving differently or because they lost a child is just crazy. Definitely not the truth at all. I have found in speaking with other women that there usually wasn't a strong relationship before the child loss. So, don't think your relationship is doomed because of your child loss. You can make it through, but both people must be willing to stick by each other's side on the bad days and the good ones. You must decide life together is better than life apart, and it must start as soon as possible. You must have the conversation and agree that you are stronger together than apart. I'm not going to pretend I know how hard it is—remember, I got divorced. But I can tell you from other families who have experienced child loss, the bond you will have together will last your entire lifetime.

I eventually met my husband, Josh, after I lost Kaleb. As I previously spoke about, he does not understand my loss and can't imagine what it's like to go through child loss. So, he doesn't try to understand it. He just listens, asks questions and shows empathy. If you have met your new love interest after your child loss, I would start by thinking about a few things. I believe still having your child in your life after they have passed is one of the most important things to tell them—I would be blunt and frank with them. The night I met Josh, he asked me if I had any children. To which I said I had a son that passed away in 2012. Not the conversation he was expecting to have but it worked out for us in the end. You need to talk about your child and tell them what to expect. I know this seems blunt, but putting a bandage on what you go through is only prolonging the truth. If someone loves you, they will have to love you for *all* of you, even on the not-so-happy days. Don't expect them to truly understand what it feels like to lose a child or understand what exactly you need. I have literally had the conversation with Josh that I need him to at least remember the days and acknowledge them. It doesn't have to be anything more than, "I'm thinking about you today." Remember, there are some people you are going to meet who are not going to be your people. Let them go—they are only blocking your perfect people from coming to you.

Parents

My parents live a quarter of a mile in front of me. They were part of Kaleb's life daily. My mom would pick him up on the way home from daycare, and we would go to my parent's house every Sunday for dinner... Old Italian traditions never die. To say Brian, my parents, and I were close is an understatement.

When Kaleb passed, my dad and mom also experienced the loss. No matter what I did, I could not change the outcome. I could not fix what happened. I try not to think about it, because when I do, it is just upsetting. They lived their life full of fun and healthy children and now, they live with the loss of Kaleb. In a day's time, they lost their normal routine and the normalcy in their life. Plus, their child was hurting— hurting badly, and no matter how much they wanted to help, they also could not fix it. It's a no-win situation all around.

I don't believe my parents have ever healed from losing Kaleb. My mom often cried about him when she talked about him, and I would find her posting on social media sometimes about him. My dad doesn't speak about Kaleb unless he is brought up, but weekly he wears a shirt that says, "Because someone I love is in heaven." My parents grieve and I don't understand it, just like they don't understand my grief. My parents and I remained close, and I still continue to visit and help my dad, as my mom passed in July of 2022.

Extended Family

Most of my extended family and I are not close, but I was surprised by the support from some and the dissociation by others. My cousin, who never goes to funerals and stays away from family outings, was the first to be by my side. He came and showed support, even though this was not typical of him. I had family I never saw come to the funeral and visit my home, but I also had some family I never heard from. Am I mad? No—and I have never really been mad about it because at first I was so numb I didn't even realize it; and now, it just doesn't matter. As I've gone through my child loss and grown as a person, I have learned that the little things just don't matter. You will learn the same, just hopefully faster than I did. My wish is for you to do better and be better than I am.

Other Children

Many of you Mommas have other children. I personally did not when I lost my Kaleb. So, you have your grief, your other half's grief, and also your other child's grief. As a Momma, you want to fix everything, as you always do. But right now, don't try to fix your family. Grieve together and just be there for each other. You have your *whole life* to try and fix everything. Now is the time just to be together.

Children grieve too, though—they don't talk about it sometimes because they don't want to upset or hurt their parents. Some may feel they need to change who they are to somehow be the missing child in the family. You may notice them changing, trying to make up for the child that is gone. Pay attention, Mommas. My biggest urge is for you to make sure you talk to your other babies. Plan family time to talk about the child you lost and the sibling they lost—this lets everyone involved know it is okay to talk about the lost child. Because a child will not want to upset you, they will feel comfortable with this time. Listen to them, as hard as it might be. Let them tell you what they are feeling or thinking. This does two things—it helps you to understand how your child is truly feeling and it allows for a new bond of trust and understanding to form.

If you are finding it is hard to talk about grief or it is being avoided in your house, set times to talk about grief. "On Friday nights at 6 p.m., we will talk for an hour about grief." Or you could choose a different day or every night—really whatever works for your situation. This allows you to open the communication with your children and your other half. As I stated earlier, children don't want to upset you and I am positive your other half does not want to hurt you, or they don't want to talk about it. Use this time to mourn together and bond over the loss. You may need to do this for months after your child loss, but eventually you will be able to talk freely about your child and feel comfortable together doing it.

I've heard some mommas say they can't even deal with their other children. I've heard other mommas say they ignore their other children and aren't giving them what they need. They say they are too crushed and emotional. Tough love moment: Momma, knock it off—now. Your children need you more now than ever. They don't expect you to be put together, but they *do* expect you to be their Momma. There is no better way to push your kids away from you than by ignoring their needs. By doing this, you could also push your older kids to use drugs and alcohol or commit crime. Your other children didn't ask for this like you didn't, so get it together.

I get so frustrated (and probably too nasty) with mommas who do this. *Talk* to your children, no matter how young they are. I started talking to my daughter as young as four when she started asking me about her brother. I tell my daughter when I'm not having a good day. And guess what? She tries to cheer me up and tells me she loves me. Sometimes she simply sits and hangs out with me, and other times she goes and does something else to give me some space. It's all about talking, Mommas. You have to talk about it. We can both agree the worst possible thing to happen is to have another child die or be lost to drugs or alcohol.

Having Another Child After Child Loss

I was one of the Mommas who had a child after my Kaleb died. She was not planned, even though I had planned to have another child— she was a surprise. I struggled when I first had Bella, because I had not dealt with grief the way I should have. My biggest fear was loving Bella and for her to be taken away from me too. I did know that she would always know about Kaleb, and I didn't want to hide Kaleb from her. I always wanted her to feel that if she wanted to talk about him, she could. She started asking about siblings way before I thought she would, at the age of four. We talked about Cayden, her stepbrother from Josh's previous marriage, and then I told her she had a brother in heaven named Kaleb. She was satisfied with that, but over the years she has wanted to talk about him. As she has gotten older, she has asked more and more about Kaleb and heaven. And as she gets older, I have explained more about what happened.

I can remember the first time she asked me how Kaleb died. I told Bella he went to sleep one night and didn't wake up. Of course, I hadn't thought it through, and it scared the hell out of her that she was going to go to sleep and not wake up. *Great job, Mom!* She actually has kids at her school who have special needs, so I explained it to her like this: Kaleb was a special needs baby. He had to fight really hard when he was born, kinda like a superhero. Because when he was born, he was sick—he wasn't healthy like you are. So, one night when he went to sleep, he went to heaven. We didn't have a problem sleeping after that. I think she was five or six at the time.

Bella is nine now, so the questioning is becoming more complex. She has asked me about Kaleb being in heaven and being alone. To which I tell her, "No." COVID took her great-grandpa and I have told her they are together along with TaTa, one of our dogs that died. I tell Bella about my grandparents and assure her: her brother is not alone. I also had to explain that Nana, my mom, was taking care of Kaleb now and watching over all of us. She finds comfort in that, I think.

Bella never met Kaleb, of course, but she still mourns him. She will come to me sometimes sad and say she misses Kaleb. Josh kinda looks at me and I just tell her that's okay, but he wouldn't want her to be sad. I wipe her tears, tell her I love her very much, and I don't want her to be sad. One time, she set up a table next to the fireplace. I have a picture of Kaleb on one half of the mantle. She laid flowers out on it and said she wanted to have a funeral for Kaleb. I told her she didn't need to do that—though I am pretty good at her talking about him and just answering the general questions, this was a little too much for me. Of course, Josh sat in silence—I don't think he knew what to say. Bella said she wanted to talk to him or something—I can't exactly remember, because it was a shock even for me. I told her, "Bella, you can talk to Kaleb anytime you want. Just talk to him and he will hear you." I told her he would always be watching over her. She said something to him, I can't remember what, and then she was done and on to the next thing.

At times like these, I often wonder if I am screwing up my kid. I wonder if I am a good mom—if I am the best person to raise her. I question my judgment; I am overprotective of her and stricter than most moms. I make her spend time with me and eat at the dinner table. I make her say, "Yes, ma'am" and "No, ma'am," or "Yes, sir" and "No, sir." But I also tell her how special she is. I tell her how no one could ever take her place. I tell her how proud I am of her and how perfect she is, just the way she is. I have found that any good momma would question whether they are a good momma. I have also found that our children aren't looking for *perfect*, they are looking for *present*. They aren't looking for the quantity of time, they are looking for quality of time. Maybe all those damn science experiments she wants to do will one day be fond memories for her. I check myself when I doubt my abilities as a mom, and you need to do the same. You are the best person to raise them and the only person that your children want. Remember that Momma.

At nine, Bella is now dealing with the loss and death of a sibling she never met. I don't cry in front of her and on days that I am upset, when she asks, I tell her Mommy doesn't feel good. To which she says, "Mommy, I hope you feel better." It makes me smile and I thank her.

Bella is such an old soul to me; she is such a special child. My worst fear is for Bella to ever feel she is inferior to Kaleb. I am so cautious of this, and when others talk about Kaleb in front of her, sometimes it makes me feel uncomfortable. I tell her daily how special she is and how I'm so very glad I'm her Momma. I urge all Mommas to let your other children know that they are perfect the way they are and *who* they are. My life would be shattered to know if later on in life she felt inferior to Kaleb. I may worry about this way too much, and maybe you worry about it too, but I just want to mention it because it's real and unavoidable.

Children today have so much they have to deal with as it is. The last thing we need to do as Mommas is bring more confusion into their life, especially at a time when they need us the most. If you can only do one thing today, hug your children and tell them you love them for who they are. Be honest with them and let them know all of you are going to be okay.

Family, friends, and children will play a role in your life after your child loss. Some will be good experiences, and some will be horrible. I wish I could tell you I didn't feel like I had the plague at times, but I did. Even sometimes today with certain people, I feel like I have the plague. Just remember that in these times, we are trying to find our new circle. The circle we find after we decide to rebuild our life will be so important in the future. We will have unbreakable bonds with them. Take each experience and be open to it, because the worst thing that can happen is you don't talk to them ever again. Keep your children close to you. On those days where you think it can't get any worse, love them even more. They won't give up on you, so you don't give up on them either.

God grant me the serenity to accept the things I cannot change, courage to change the things I can, and the wisdom to know the difference, living one day at a time: enjoying one moment at a time.

–Serenity Prayer

Chapter 7:

Spirituality and Signs

It's amazing how you can overlook things or even not consider the value of things until way later in your journey through child loss. All I kept thinking about was how no one could take care of Kaleb the way I could. Not even God. He was my child, and I was supposed to be taking care of him. I kept my mind worrying about Kaleb and what he was doing. I worried about if he was getting what he needed because, even though he was gone, the mom in me still worried about my Kaleb.

Instead of worrying about my emotions, my eating, or my living, I was still stuck on being Kaleb's mom. Those first few weeks, I thought about this constantly. I was consumed by the thought and had anxiety about Kaleb. I am not sure why, but if this has happened to you, just know you're not alone.

Remember from the previous chapters, God and I were not on speaking terms. I was pissed at him and couldn't believe I had to go through this. It wasn't fair, and I was playing the victim's role. Something had to happen—and though I thought I was fine; I was losing my mind without even knowing it. And something *did* happen which changed aspects of my grief.

Dreams

One night, I don't know how, but I fell asleep. As I was deep in sleep Kaleb came to me. I remember standing in a field looking around; and as I looked ahead of me, I saw Kaleb running toward me. When he reached me, he grabbed onto my legs, hugging them tightly. As I leaned over to look at him smiling, he looked up at me with those big, beautiful eyes and smiled back. And that was the end of the dream. No talking, I didn't hug him, and it was over in a split second. I remember waking up the next day and telling Brian about the dream. He listened, though I'm not sure if he half believed me or not. But it was real, and I actually remembered the dream. The dream gave me a sense of peace and an unimaginable calming effect on me.

That dream was a symbol of everything I worried about with Kaleb's death. He was running, he was smiling, and he could look up at me. As I mentioned before, Kaleb had cerebral palsy when he was here with me. This disability left him in a wheelchair, where he did not have use of his legs or arms. He was running to me, and he could use his legs and his arms now, as he had wrapped his arms around me and hugged my legs. When Kaleb would smile, he would always turn his head to the side and have a grin on his face; but in my dream, he looked up at me and smiled the biggest smile. Kaleb also was nearsighted and had cortical blindness, so he wore glasses to correct some of his vision. He could never see clearly like we could, but he could see a little. In my dream, when he looked up at me, he was not wearing his glasses. He could *see*.

Looking back on that dream, it was Kaleb's way of telling me he was okay. It was his way of telling me he was going to be okay and to stop worrying. I know some people don't believe in signs and it was just a dream, but I've held this dream close to my heart ever since. I have never dreamed about Kaleb again. Just that one time in the first weeks after Kaleb had passed. Sometimes I wish he would come to me again, just so I can see him and remember; but I am thankful for the dream I did have.

Nightmares

I will say—even with all of the good signs and that dream, I still have nightmares. My nightmares are about Bella, and they usually come about from one of my triggers—vacation. Working in law enforcement so long, I have seen things I can't take back, and I have seen evil at its worst. My nightmares wake me up sweating, and sometimes I can't breathe. Sometimes they are so real I have to touch Bella to make sure she is still there. My fear is about something horrible happening to her. Kidnapping and drowning are the two I dream about the most—and all because we plan a vacation. This is a time when most people relax, but my anxiety goes through the roof—one because of my job and the other, because I already lost Kaleb. I don't want to lose her too.

Not all dreams are going to be fluffy. Not all experiences will be exactly what you imagined, but I want you to remember this: Every time I have one of these episodes or one of these thoughts, I say out loud, "No I am not going to think like this, God please let me stop dreaming about this, this will not happen." I'm not sure if you experience nightmares too, but if you do, please know you are not alone. Though my nightmares are about vacation, your nightmares can be about anything. Yours could be about the incident, or the night that your child died—whatever it is, I know how real they can be.

If you experience a nightmare, try talking out loud, telling yourself what you have just experienced is not real. Start to think of something positive. Mommas, take a deep breath; and if you must, get up and walk around. Sometimes I must get up and walk to get water, to get my mind on something else for a moment. It allows me to reset my mind. There are a few times I can count on one hand that no matter what I did, I could not stop thinking about what I had just dreamed about. When I have those nights, I will get on social media and within an hour, I can usually go back to sleep.

You may have problems sleeping, but to recharge your brain and be able to deal with each day optimistically, you definitely need sleep. I know it's hard to hear this right now, as I am sure some of you just aren't sleeping at all. I hope you can return to a sleep cycle soon.

I don't know if you believe in signs that your child is with you or not, but I do believe that our children are always around us. This is coming from a realist too, by the way. I think all we have to do is ask. All we have to do is talk to them, because they are always listening.

Spirituality

When I was starting my journey of figuring out who I was and what I wanted, I still did not have my faith back with God. I spent so much energy running from Him and wanting to hear nothing about Him. Please know this isn't a book about how God changed my life at all. I believe we choose what path we walk, and we are given decisions. Each decision leads us down a different path—some good and some bad. But when it came to Kaleb, I had to learn that Kaleb was my gift from God and that I was allowed to be his mom for only a short time. I had to remember that God himself understood my suffering because he gave his son for our sins as well. God has felt our pain, Mommas, he knows our suffering.

I am not one to preach church, and I rarely talk about my beliefs, but I want you ladies to know what I was thinking for you to think about it too. As for those Mommas who don't believe in God, what does your belief say? What does your spirituality believe about children who die? I don't know, and I am not going to try and pretend I do, Mommas. Just remember what your belief says about a child passing. I do not judge anyone for their belief because it is not my place, so please know these are just my thoughts.

I believe in heaven and hell, and I believe Kaleb is waiting for me. I believe I will see him again and that it will be a wonderful, joyous day. That is what makes Kaleb and I being apart bearable. As much as I didn't believe that back when I started this journey, now I know I still have so much more that I am to do here on Earth. I know that I am here to raise Bella to be a great human and guide her. I know I am here to help the hundreds (or even thousands) of Mommas who pick up this book or join my Facebook group or coaching program. Maybe, Mommas, this journey you are going down is meant for you to tell your story—to find your path. I know, what the freak ever, but what if it truly is?

Signs

When I first started my rebuild, I was told that my Kaleb would always be around. Did I believe it? Hell no, but each day he leaves signs for me. Again, I promise I am not crazy, but I have experienced them often.

I remember when Bella was younger—probably around four—she would play in her room and was always talking. One day, out of curiosity, I asked her who she was talking to. Bella told me she was talking to her friend and her friend didn't have a name, but he was a boy. She wasn't scared of her friend, and one day I just asked her what he looked like. She really couldn't tell me, but she did say he had glasses. My heart dropped and I showed her a picture of Kaleb and asked her if that was her friend. She could not say one way or the other—but to this day, I like to believe it was Kaleb. Bella doesn't mention her friend anymore or even talk about her old friend, but I like to believe it was Kaleb who wanted to spend some time with her.

Signs are all around us, Mommas. Just like the morning I got home from the hospital, after Kaleb's death—the deer just walking out of nowhere to have a staring contest with me. I do live in the country, but that stuff just doesn't happen all the time. A deer is thought to symbolize gentleness, unconditional love, and mindfulness. And here was this beautiful doe standing within 50 feet from me staring back at me.

A recent sign I heard about was that numbers in sets of threes, meaning three consecutive numbers in a row, was a sign from loved ones. This month when I got my phone bill, it was $333.04. Yes, don't talk about my phone bill—we have a lot of people under our plan. So then, I looked up the symbolic meaning of 333. Just a quick search on PsychNewsDaily revealed, "your guardian angel is beside you to provide you with the strength and ability to take one step" (Burnett, 2023).

The very first symbol I heard about was that when dragonflies are nearby, this is a sign our loved ones are near. Dragonflies are said to symbolize change and transformation. Around seven years ago, I could go on my front porch at any given time and see dragonflies all around. I still see some, but not as many as I did before. As I started writing this chapter, one sat with me on my chair. No shit—took a video and picture of him for proof.

Cardinals are often talked about as being signs of your loved ones being around. Two years ago, I would look out my kitchen window and there were at least a dozen in the bushes. I didn't feed them at the time, but they were eating something out of the bushes. I have a bird feeder now with cardinal bird seed in it, so I still see a few from time to time. I chalk that summer two years ago up to me needing them around.

No, Mommas, I don't see ghosts and I don't believe that spirits walk the halls of my house. I don't believe in chills meaning a spirit passes through you. I do get truly freaked out by ghost stories and scary movies. Though I do believe that if we ask and we truly pay attention, we have signs all around us. You may have already experienced your child trying to let you know they are still with you.

As I questioned starting my Facebook group, my coaching program, and the writing of this book, I spoke out to Kaleb and to God to give me a sign this was right. I felt a calling, but on the flip side, pouring out my soul and being so vulnerable as an introvert scared me. It still makes me uneasy, but I asked for a sign, something so I knew. I would think it and speak it.

The first time I saw a sign that I was on the right path was when I was coming home from my parents' house and a cardinal flew in front of my vehicle. It didn't seem like much of a sign at the time, so I blew it off. The second time, I was sitting in my car and a cardinal landed on my driver-side mirror and kept jumping from my mirror to my window and back again. He did it for a while until I rolled down my window—I guess I thought I was Mary Poppins, and he was going to come and perch himself on my finger; but needless to say, he flew off. I did manage to record a video of the cardinal doing this before I chased him away by rolling down the window. It's still posted as a Reel on my Instagram account. The third time was a cardinal again, and this time he came to the passenger side mirror as Bella and I were walking up to the house. He was going from my mirror to my window, back and forth. Bella was in awe, and I finally said out loud, "Okay, I get it."

As I said earlier in this chapter, a dragonfly landed on my chair and stayed around, even after poking at him. Of course, I posted that video to my Instagram Reels too. Hand raised, I promise we don't have an animal farm and raise dragonflies and cardinals. I just opened my mind up to the possibility of having these interactions.

Do I believe in psychics and mediums? Nope, not at all—though I do find them fascinating. I know exactly why I don't: I have trust issues. I have always been standoffish with individuals I don't know. And this also goes hand in hand with ghosts and spirits being around freaking me out. These are just my thoughts, just my opinion—and my opinion is not based on facts. If you want to see a psychic or a medium, I am all for you doing it because the truth is: No one, not even me, should be telling you how to move forward and how to rebuild your life. As I have said a lot—you do you. I do warn you to be careful, though. It should be mentioned that many people take advantage of us in our most vulnerable state. They will steal your joy and steal all they can get from you. Sad that I even must mention this, but it happens daily.

In this chapter, I just chose to touch on signs and spirituality because this is a pretty touchy subject—not that I am afraid of angering anyone, but because I don't want you to believe what I believe. I want you to form your own opinions and speak your truth with your testimony.

I do believe that you still need to have hope. My beliefs are in line with seeing my Kaleb one day, where yours may not be. Whatever it is that you believe, that is okay. For myself, I choose to believe that I will see my Kaleb again. It is what keeps me going on the hard days and I will say—the longer I have gone through my child loss, the less I think about it. I just know in my heart I will see him.

I want all of you to sit down and have a true discussion with yourself on what you believe and what you will allow yourself to believe. This will allow you to accept the signs when they come. Know that you and your beliefs are part of this journey. Find out who you are in every aspect of your life. Be who you are and whatever you feel, be proud of it. You don't have to justify your beliefs to anyone. You don't even have to tell them; you just know and be firm in your beliefs.

The reality is that you will grieve forever. You will not 'get over' the loss of a loved one; you will learn to live with it. You will heal and you will rebuild yourself around the loss you have suffered. You will be whole again, but you will never be the same. Nor should you be the same nor would you want to.

–Elisabeth Kübler-Ross

Chapter 8:

Expect the Unexpected

You know the saying, "This is a catchall"? I guess you can consider this chapter a "catchall." There are so many things that go on in child loss and they make absolutely no sense—and you wonder why this is happening right now, in this moment. This is the chapter of little things that make up the huge things in the whole picture of child loss. Things that we go through and think only happen to us. They don't happen to all of us, but are still worth mentioning. I want you Mommas to know that it does happen and to know, it happened to me too—you are not alone.

I truly believed and worried about Kaleb not being taken care of when he passed. In my mind, I always felt no one could take care of Kaleb the way I could. No one would know the ins and outs of his day; no one could possibly understand my child the way I did. Not even God. I missed taking care of Kaleb and worried for days, he wasn't getting exactly what he needed. It's hard to believe, but this was me.

Maybe you didn't feel this way, or maybe you did. I lost all faith in God, and maybe that was why I worried so much in the early days of my child loss. We are Mommas, and we are built to protect and guard our children. We would do *anything* to keep them safe. When this is torn away from us, we worry. We worry because we are Mommas. Don't try to make sense of it, this is just natural. You can choose to stop worrying, though. Keep telling yourself that your child is safe, they have everything they could possibly need, and they are being taken care of until you see them again. This isn't something you tell yourself one time and it works, though. If you have learned anything thus far, I hope it is that you must repeat little steps like these over and over again.

The Little Sentimental Things

I think it's the little things after the loss of my Kaleb that I realize were insignificant to most people—but for me, they were the most important. These things can be something as simple as a lunch box. A lunch box, right? I lost my mind about the lunch box that we kept all of Kaleb's medication in.

As I mentioned previously, Kaleb took medication daily. Instead of keeping the medication out on the counter, we kept it all in a Superman lunch box next to the dry-erase board, which had his medication schedule on it. Although we would never forget Kaleb's medication schedule after the first few weeks, it was organization and something I could control at a time when chaos reigned. As I told you earlier, I gave Kaleb's medication to the Paramedics who came to our house, which is a standard procedure for medical emergencies. When we left the hospital, I forgot to ask them for it. Once I remembered, I had to have it back—it was *his*. I remember telling my parents I had to get it back because it was Kaleb's. We called the hospital and begged them to find it, telling them that though we didn't need his medication anymore, it held sentimental value. We did end up getting the lunch box back—the hospital had kept it, just in case.

Something of sentimental value to Brian was Kaleb's glasses. When Brian and I separated, he wanted Kaleb's glasses. We had two different pairs, an everyday pair and his nice glasses when he would take pictures and go places. I never asked him why, but to him, he had to have them—it meant something to him. To this day, I am sure he still has them in a special place where he can pull them out and remember.

Little things like these examples above mean the most when you lose your child. We want to hold on to everything because we can't physically hold on to our child, so we seek anything physical that we can touch and see. This could be something owned by your child, to make us feel close to them. Something like this can be extremely upsetting, make you sad, or put you in a fit of rage. Understand this is normal and okay to feel. It is us who want to continue to have something physical of our angels. It is a way for us to control something from a situation that was completely out of our control.

To this day, I still sleep with one of Kaleb's baby blankets at night. It goes with me wherever I lay my head down—vacation, work training, you name it. I remember Josh asking me one time about it. I told him it was Kaleb's and I slept with it. That was all it took, as he knows, and the blanket is to remain guarded and cherished on the bed away from any dog who may try to chew on it. I don't care *who* knows I sleep with a baby blanket as a 40-plus-year-old woman. It's not about others, it's about me; and in the beginning, this helped me find the comfort I needed to get through the endless nights and days. It was my way of having my son close, even though he was gone. It was being able to physically hold something that was so close to him at one time. The smell of my son gradually over time is gone, but it is still my physical piece of Kaleb that I can hold. In the first months of my child loss, it gave me so much comfort. Now, it is still comforting, but I don't need it in the same way I first did.

Find a comfort that makes your child feel close to you. It may be a baby blanket, an item of clothing, glasses, a lunch box, a bracelet, or many other things. When you find yourself lonely (which you will) or you need to feel close to your child, pull it out. Remember the good times wrapped around that physical thing. Remember your child— when they laughed, when they spoke, or when they made you proud. Hold on to that physical thing until you don't need it anymore for comfort. I am not saying throw it away, but I am saying keep it close until you can store it away somewhere safe.

I also have a necklace I bought within weeks of Kaleb dying, and a ring I bought later. The necklace was a blue cameo of a mother holding a young child. I placed it on a chain and wore it every day up until year eight. It never came off until one day, the chain broke. Again, as I have discussed before, I am not a signs kind of person, but I did take it as a sign. Bella had already been born, and it made me wonder when she got older if she would think that Kaleb was above her. Or if in some way, she would feel inferior to Kaleb. I still don't know the answer to this question, but I did not buy another chain to place the cameo on, though I have it kept in my jewelry box. I will have it until I pass on, and I can take it out anytime I want to remember.

Lastly, I bought a ring as well. It is rose gold and has a purple stone in it, but I did not spend an extreme amount of money on it. I bought it as my reminder of the most important things in life. I came to a point in my journey (really early on, within a few months) where I realized family was the most important thing in life. I always had this vision that me succeeding as a female would be the most significant event in my life. I thought that my life would be measured by how many degrees I earned and how much I broke the mold of, "You can't do that." Once I lost Kaleb, though, I would have given back my degree and my success in law enforcement. I knew I would never make Bella think that a job was more important than her. I vowed never to put my job before my family. Don't get me wrong, I was never the one who chose a job over family—but I still had the mindset that I had to be powerful as a woman in order to show my worth. I don't think I would have ever forgotten to put my family first, but the ring I wear around my finger always reminds me.

These little things help us accept that even though our child is not with us, they are still near. It might seem like this will not work for you (and that it's possibly a dumb notion), but the idea of having your child near you by using a certain item does trick your brain. No, of course, you won't forget that your child is gone; no, you won't wake up one day and be fine with everything. It is a silent reminder to those thoughts you are thinking about in the back of your brain—your child is always with you. I urge you to try it, what will it hurt?

The Paperwork

Another thing that really doesn't have a place in a chapter, that I want you to be aware of, is all the paperwork that goes along with the death of your child. Not just the funeral paperwork, but all the other paperwork you work months after your child loss to complete. Sign this paper, take their name off this paperwork, cancel this appointment, notify this person of their death or that doctor... This takes weeks, if not months, to fill out and notify—and once you think you are done, there are yet more things you must do. I wish there was an easier way to do it—you could get someone to help you, but sometimes this is something the parents have to do all on their own. It's part of the child loss journey, and one that will be very emotional. Just know that all of it does not need to be done in one day, or in one week. Do it as you can, and eventually it will all be done.

Kaleb died in March of 2012. During tax season in January of 2013, we claimed Kaleb as our child for the last time. The past nine months were a roller coaster of emotion, but this was the last thing. We filed our taxes and waited for them to be approved, as everyone does, only to be flagged weeks later because someone else had claimed Kaleb on their taxes. I shit you not... unbelievably, someone had claimed my Kaleb on their taxes. We were violated and the emotions came pouring out. But mostly we felt anger and I wanted justice for this—I wanted someone to pay for doing such a cruel and shocking act. How could someone be keeping track of people—a child, dying—and hope they would not be claimed? Just to make an easy dollar on the death of a child. My gosh, there is a special place in hell for people out there like this. It happens, and it happened to us.

We did all of the paperwork like we were supposed to, we did everything and checked every box, but someone still took advantage of a horrific situation. So instead of things flowing and allowing us just to move through this last step, we had to prove that Kaleb was our son and had to send the IRS his death certificate. We had to explain the situation to multiple people over the next few days, reliving his death again by fighting to prove he was our son. Such a crappy position to be in, but as I now realize, there are horrible people everywhere. They will take advantage of you when you are at your weakest. So be strong and make it through these trying times.

No one was ever held accountable for the fraud, and the IRS did not care because it was not enough money for them to do anything but file a report and move on. Which is fine, I understand that it is not the type of money to put someone in jail for. BUT, it mattered to us. We knew someone at our health department took advantage of Kaleb's death certificate coming across their desk. We *still* know people are making money off of the death of children every year, and it is sickening.

I had to learn that things I hold so important to me are not valued similarly by others. I had to remember that as months and years went on, and I still remind myself of this each year when it is Kaleb's death date or Kaleb's birthday. Most people will forget—and Mommas, that is okay. You remember, and those closest to you remember.

Think about the last time you had to stop for a funeral procession. You stop and wait and wait, wondering possibly how much longer it would be; or you may have wondered what happened or if they were a child. But once the procession is done, you continue on with your day. The incident will soon be forgotten by you; but for those involved, it may be a lasting roller coaster of emotion like you have dealt with. To you, it is not an important part of your life; but to those involved, it means the world to them. That is how you must think about it. Not everyone will get it and for them, life moves on. Don't hate them because of this, instead choose to have them in your life or remove them from your life. Your life is precious, and wasting time on those who are not on the same page as you can lessen the joy you experience. You have learned life is short, and it's about surrounding yourself with your people.

Triggers and Karens

My mom passing in July of 2022 would become an event that was unexpected. She was really sick for the last two weeks before her death, and we knew she had heart problems as her heart was only functioning at 23%. She passed away at home after Bella and I had left for gymnastics. While at gymnastics, she passed away within 15 minutes of the class starting. It is truly heartbreaking what you do in the days to come after someone dies. It was the same process that I went through with Kaleb; but now, I was helping my dad navigate it. I had dealt with death since the loss of Kaleb with family and a friend, but I was not expecting to feel the emotions of losing Kaleb at that particular point.

What I noticed in the days to come was me again grieving the loss of my Kaleb. This was something I had not had a problem with for years, minus the few bad days a year. I did not understand it—I had passed this point a long time ago. I cried, *boy* did I cry—not only for my mom, but for Kaleb. I missed him so much and I needed him.

As I have learned to do, and as I spoke about earlier in this book, I began to break down my emotions and discover what exactly was causing the sudden grief again over losing Kaleb. I began to break it down. I knew any death could cause my grief to resurface, but I felt there was more to it because I had lost someone close to me before. Even so, it seemed there was more to what I was experiencing. I felt it had something to do with my mom, something even more than the grief from losing her. I started to think about the past when my mom was with Kaleb, and I thought about my mom since Kaleb had passed. I thought about how much everything had changed, and what big changes had happened since his passing. Then I knew what it was. My life at the present day is filled daily with many wonderful people, but I may run into one person who remembers me as Kaleb's mom or remembers when he was alive. Most remember my memories of him.

My mom was there with Kaleb from the beginning. She lived his traumatic birth, she lived his daily life, and she was there during his death. My mom was an actual living person who knew Kaleb physically, but now she was gone. In a sense, when she passed, some of Kaleb's memory passed with her. It was one more person who had passed who knew Kaleb from more than just stories and my memories. She had moments and her own memories of times with Kaleb, not just my memories. That is what hurt so bad with my mom's death. I felt that another piece of Kaleb died along with her.

I have learned how to understand my triggers, and I understand that I will never again revert to who I was in the first years that I lost Kaleb; but that doesn't mean I don't have moments when I worry I am slipping back down that road again. If you find yourself having more bad days than good and you have just a completely awful day or week, it's time to sit back down and evaluate where this is coming from. To know where it is coming from is so powerful. It's you, Momma, taking control of your loss and reminding yourself that your life is not going to be defined by your child loss. You are stronger and more powerful than you can ever imagine.

Lastly, I want to tell you a story about a donkey, a mom, and a daughter. It was originally about a donkey, a man, and a son; but we are all women (girl power) so we are changing the story's characters. A mom, a daughter, and a donkey are walking to town.

The mom and daughter are walking beside the donkey and as they pass a group of Karens, the group of Karens make rude comments about why they would have a donkey and not ride it. So, the mom and the daughter stop, and the mom gets on the donkey. They go a little way and there is another group of Karens. This time they are making rude comments about the mom making the daughter walk and how wrong it is. So, the mom and the daughter stop, and the daughter gets on the donkey and the mom walks. They go a little way and come in contact with another group of Karens. These Karens are making rude comments about the daughter and how she's making her poor mother walk, as the mother is so much older. So, the mom and the daughter stop, and both the mom and the daughter get on the donkey and continue to town. They ride a little longer and come in contact with another group of Karens. These Karens begin to make rude comments about the mom and the daughter for putting too much weight on the donkey and how wrong they are to do so. So, the mom and the daughter get down, make a makeshift stretcher, and carry the donkey. As they are walking, they come in contact with another group of Karens, and they are making rude comments about how dumb it is to have a fine donkey, yet they are carrying it. The story ends with the stretcher breaking, the donkey falling into the water, and drowning.

Can you think of the moral of the story? No matter what you do, there is always going to be a group of Karens telling you how you are doing it wrong and how you should really do it. You can't, and you won't, please everyone in life.

I love that story because I think about it like our child loss. There is always going to be that group of people who think you should be reacting a certain way to your loss. There is always going to be that group of people (or a person) who think you should do more or less to heal. There are going to be people who don't even know you, yet still try to tell you how to handle your child loss. Stop trying to please all of them. Stop trying to make everyone happy—because right now, Momma, it is all about you. It isn't about what everyone else thinks you should or should not be doing. It's not about how long someone thinks you should be grieving your child loss. It is about you and your grieving, and how you adapt and move on with your memories. It's about you keeping what's good to you and what you like, and throwing away all that garbage you don't want to do or don't need anymore.

This is the rebuild of your life, and the only one steering the ship is you. You have lived your worst day; your morals, values, and beliefs have changed. Don't let the Karens' opinion take up any of your time. Ignore them and move past them—they are not your people, and that is absolutely fine. It's time to move forward and grow for your own sake.

I believe in being strong when everything seems to be going wrong. I believe that happy girls are the prettiest girls. I believe tomorrow is another day, and I believe in miracles. –Audrey Hepburn

Chapter 9:

What Is in Your Future?

Are we really to the last chapter? In this book, yes, but it is the beginning of the most powerful rebuild in your life—so no. Although your child loss has broken you, the rebuilding of your life and finding purpose will be equally challenging. But you have it in you, Momma, life is yours and will give to you if you ask of it.

Willpower—one definition of this word is "strong determination that allows one to do something difficult" (Merriam-Webster, 2023). When we lose our child, the easiest thing to do is sink—sink in our emotions and live forever with this deep sorrow. It is what our body tells us to do, it is what people blurt out to us when they say, "I don't know how you do it." It is our society and how we are molded when we are told how the life cycle goes. We broke that mold when our child died. So, who are we?

I refuse to believe after everything we have been through that our life ends the day our child dies. I refuse to believe our lives are defined by a single event that would cause us to hit our lowest; because what are we told, Mommas? We are told all the time that when we reach our lowest point, we are opening ourselves up for greatness. Of course, no one was ever thinking about child loss; but what if we changed our mindset to include child loss too? What could we do? What could we be?

I remember hitting my lowest point and not caring if I lived or where my life was going. I did not care about much at all. I just knew I wanted to be with my Kaleb—that would be my happy place. I played the victim, the victim of child loss; I expected the world to understand and was shocked when the world told me it was time to forget my son. It wasn't that they *wanted* me to forget my Kaleb, they just wanted me to push Kaleb to the back of my thoughts, so *they* did not have to deal with child loss. The world kept moving, but my world stopped the day Kaleb died. I danced the victim dance for a long time... until I realized I was dancing alone. I had to hit the bottom, nowhere I had ever been or have ever gone since. I had to have the willpower to say, "I am not going to live like this forever." Once I realized that, I had to have the strength and the courage to pick myself back up. I had to find the strength within me, strength I did not know I even had. But there was one problem—after recognizing what I needed to do, I had to take that next step and I did not know what that looked like.

Your old life that you once lived is no more. You are not broken or damaged goods, you are a Momma who is about to tackle life without your child. The next steps in your life are all up to you. No one is coming to save you from yourself, and no one can help you with your loss. I, like others, can only guide you and tell you that you are not alone; and I can share with you what I have learned to deal with it every day. Like others before you, I made the one decision that changed the outcome of my life. I decided to live and find a purpose for who I was becoming. After I made that decision, I never looked back.

Start with the yes and tell yourself "I am going to be more and become more." Start with your story and follow those steps I have mentioned in the earlier chapters. You want to figure out what rebuilding and finding purpose means to you. Each of us will find a purpose and rebuild our lives differently. Go back to the beginning, as we have spoken about—your values and beliefs have probably changed. What are your values and what are your beliefs? They are two totally different things. If you value family, what specific aspects of family do you value—the love or closeness? What is it for you? Digging deep down to the core of who you are helps you to understand where you are at. The traumatic event you just experienced has changed your values and beliefs. This step is so important to understand, Mommas. This is because understanding you are not who you were helps you understand the phrase, "I just want my life to go back to normal," is not possible. Once you understand that, you realize that you are starting as a blank slate, per se. Any guilt or regret can be demolished because you are not that person you once were. Anything negative you have held on to, let it go–today is a new start.

Rebuild your life the way you want it to be. No one else matters but your angel child. If you are like me, it matters even less how others feel about you at this point in your life. Those that knew you before your child loss have no idea how you have grown as a person, unless they have stood by you since the loss of your child. Opinions of others don't matter because firstly, they aren't as strong as you are and secondly, they will never understand the willpower and courage it takes for you to say, "I am not my child loss".

Stop waiting for the perfect date and time. There is no certain number of weeks or months to wait before starting to rebuild and find purpose in your life. The truth is, it's our way of pushing it off whether you know that or not. The sooner you start to understand your loss, the sooner you will be able to begin rebuilding your life. Decide today that you want to rebuild your life. Decide today that you want to find peace. It is that one small step that can change the outcome of your life forever. Stop telling yourself you can't and start telling yourself you *will*. Momma, if you don't believe it, hear me when I tell you: You are strong and you are special. We will never know why we were chosen, why we must walk a life without our child; so, stop wondering because there will never be an answer. Yes, I am going to say it: If you live in your child loss, you are not living. That is not living, Momma—and deep down, you know this. You don't want to feel the way you are feeling. Affirm this today: I am strong, I am special. I have the willpower.

Your decision to rebuild your life and find peace has absolutely nothing to do with forgetting your child. Your child should always remain a piece of you and your life. I said early on in this book that your life is like a book. It is filled with many chapters. One of the main characters in your book was your child. It is filled with many great times, and then the worst time—your child loss. As you move through your next chapters, remember that the first chapters where your child was with you have not been erased. Those chapters are still part of who you are. Like any book, the main character—your child—is still mentioned and part of the story. They no longer play a major role, but they are still part of what makes up your life, and your book. They will remain a chapter until you are with your child again.

I want to give you a word to think about: Vilomah (said like Vee-loh-mah). It means against the natural order. We can all agree, we definitely are living against the natural order. So, if we are living against natural order, why would we follow anyone's view on child loss but our own? We will live the rest of our lives with our loss, so let's choose to live it our way. Be who you want to be and do what you want to do, because that is what life is about. Until now, you may have been blind to all the shiny objects in life; but now, more than ever, you know that life can be exactly what you make it. Live against the natural order in everything you do. I know I love the shock factor, and so should you. Be exactly who you are and who you want to be. *Free* yourself, Mommas.

Many people who have lost children say they hate the phrase, "Everything happens for a reason," but I truly believe in this phrase. Everything that happens to us in life does happen for a reason. That phrase is not saying that it all has to be wonderful. "What reason could possibly be a good reason for a child to die?" I don't have the answer, and I stopped pondering this a long time ago. All I know is this: I am a better version of myself, and I know the true meaning of living life to its fullest. I know that the night Kaleb was born after a complete placental abruption and losing 3 1/2 pints of blood I am still here; and I know 11 years later, I have survived child loss. I know I can't imagine my life without my Bella in it. I can't imagine not taking care of my dad after my mom passed away. I refuse to believe my child loss was my whole life; it will always play a huge part in my life, though, and who I have become.

I truly don't know how to end this book, but I will end it by saying this: We did not choose to live the life we were dealt, but we have the choice not to live in it forever. There is no written rule that our life was supposed to be easy. We are not guaranteed to have happy lives free of pain. That is a fairy tale that we have been fed our whole life, and maybe to an extent we believed it up until our child loss. What I do know is that for us living in child loss, we have the strength to pick ourselves up. All we have to do is find our willpower and courage.

Much love to you, Momma. Please know I am always thinking of you and every Momma battling the journey of child loss. It is my hope that this book helps you to rebuild your life while lovingly honoring your angel baby. You are worthy of happiness, and you are stronger than you believe. Be brave, my warriors.

References

Auguilera, Christina. (1999 November 28). What a Girl Wants. Genius. **https://genius.com/Christina-aguilera-what-a-girl-wants-lyrics**

Burnett, Daria. (2023 February 8). 333 Angel Number Meaning: What does 333 mean in love spirituality, and numerology. Psych New Daily. **https://www.psychnewsdaily.com/the-333-angel-number-meaning-at-once-helpful-and-heavenly/**

Lach's Legacy. (2020 July 2). Can our marriage survive the death of our child. **https://www.lachslegacy.org/blog/2022/7/2/can-our-marriage-survive-the-death-of-our-child#:~:text=Newer%20data%20shows%20that%20only, be%20polarizing%20for%20a%20couple**.

Merrien-Webster. (2023 May 8). Willpower. **https://www.merriam-webster.com/dictionary/willpower**

Recover for Grief. (2020, May 30). 7 Stages of Grief-Going Through the Process and Back to Life. **https://www.recover-from-grief.com/7-stages-of-grief.html**

Made in the USA
Middletown, DE
18 June 2025

77195552R00076